THE CAMBRIDGE BIBLE COMMENTARY

NEW ENGLISH BIBLE

GENERAL EDITORS

P. R. ACKROYD, A. R. C. LEANEY, J. W. PACKER

JEREMIAH 1–25

THE BOOK OF THE PROPHET
JEREMIAH
CHAPTERS 1–25

COMMENTARY BY

ERNEST W. NICHOLSON

Lecturer in Divinity at the University of Cambridge
Fellow and Dean of Pembroke College

CAMBRIDGE

AT THE UNIVERSITY PRESS

1973

Published by the Syndics of the Cambridge University Press
Bentley House, 200 Euston Road, London NW1 2DB
American Branch: 32 East 57th Street, New York, N.Y.10022

© Cambridge University Press 1973

Library of Congress Catalogue Card Number: 73–80477

ISBNS
0 521 08625 6 hard covers
0 521 09769 x paperback

Printed in Great Britain
at the University Printing House, Cambridge
(Brooke Crutchley, University Printer)

To

M. B. D.

in affection and esteem

GENERAL EDITORS' PREFACE

The aim of this series is to provide the text of the New English Bible closely linked to a commentary in which the results of modern scholarship are made available to the general reader. Teachers and young people have been especially kept in mind. The commentators have been asked to assume no specialized theological knowledge, and no knowledge of Greek and Hebrew. Bare references to other literature and multiple references to other parts of the Bible have been avoided. Actual quotations have been given as often as possible.

The completion of the New Testament part of the series in 1967 provides a basis upon which the production of the much larger Old Testament and Apocrypha series can be undertaken. The welcome accorded to the series has been an encouragement to the editors to follow the same general pattern, and an attempt has been made to take account of criticisms which have been offered. One necessary change is the inclusion of the translators' footnotes since in the Old Testament these are more extensive, and essential for the understanding of the text.

Within the severe limits imposed by the size and scope of the series, each commentator will attempt to set out the main findings of recent biblical scholarship and to describe the historical background to the text. The main theological issues will also be critically discussed.

Much attention has been given to the form of the volumes. The aim is to produce books each of which will be read consecutively from first to last page. The introductory material leads naturally into the text, which itself leads into the alternating sections of the commentary.

The series is accompanied by three volumes of a more general character. *Understanding the Old Testament* sets out to provide the larger historical and archaeological background, to say something about the life and thought of the people of the Old Testament, and to answer the question 'Why should we study the Old Testament?'. *The Making of the Old Testament* is concerned with the formation of the books of the Old Testament and Apocrypha in the context of the ancient near eastern world, and with the ways in which these books have come down to us in the life of the Jewish and Christian communities. *Old Testament Illustrations* contains maps, diagrams and photographs with an explanatory text. These three volumes are designed to provide material helpful to the understanding of the individual books and their commentaries, but they are also prepared so as to be of use quite independently.

P. R. A.
A. R. C. L.
J. W. P.

CONTENTS

THE FOOTNOTES TO THE
N.E.B. TEXT

The footnotes to the N.E.B. text are designed to help the reader either to understand particular points of detail – the meaning of a name, the presence of a play upon words – or to give information about the actual text. Where the Hebrew text appears to be erroneous, or there is doubt about its precise meaning, it may be necessary to turn to manuscripts which offer a different wording, or to ancient translations of the text which may suggest a better reading, or to offer a new explanation based upon conjecture. In such cases, the footnotes supply very briefly an indication of the evidence, and whether the solution proposed is one that is regarded as possible or as probable. Various abbreviations are used in the footnotes.

(1) Some abbreviations are simply of terms used in explaining a point: *ch(s).*, chapter(s); *cp.*, compare; *lit.*, literally; *mng.*, meaning; *MS(S).*, manuscript(s), i.e. Hebrew manuscript(s), unless otherwise stated; *om.*, omit(s); *or*, indicating an alternative interpretation; *poss.*, possible; *prob.*, probable; *rdg.*, reading; *Vs(s).*, version(s).

(2) Other abbreviations indicate sources of information from which better interpretations or readings may be obtained.

Aq. Aquila, a Greek translator of the Old Testament (perhaps about A.D. 130) characterized by great literalness.

Aram. Aramaic – may refer to the text in this language (used in parts of Ezra and Daniel), or to the meaning of an Aramaic word. Aramaic belongs to the same language family as Hebrew, and is known from about 1000 B.C. over a wide area of the Middle East, including Palestine.

Heb. Hebrew – may refer to the Hebrew text or may indicate the literal meaning of the Hebrew word.

Josephus Flavius Josephus (A.D. 37/8–about 100), author of the *Jewish Antiquities*, a survey of the whole history of his people, directed partly at least to a non-Jewish audience, and of various other works, notably one on the *Jewish War* (that of A.D. 66–73) and a defence of Judaism (*Against Apion*).

Luc. Sept. Lucian's recension of the Septuagint, an important edition made in Antioch in Syria about the end of the third century A.D.

Pesh. Peshitta or Peshitto, the Syriac version of the Old Testament. Syriac is the name given chiefly to a form of Eastern Aramaic used by the Christian community. The translation varies in quality, and is at many points influenced by the Septuagint or the Targums.

Sam.   Samaritan Pentateuch – the form of the first five books of the Old Testament as used by the Samaritan community. It is written in Hebrew in a special form of the Old Hebrew script, and preserves an important form of the text, somewhat influenced by Samaritan ideas.

Scroll(s)   Scroll(s), commonly called the Dead Sea Scrolls, found at or near Qumran from 1947 onwards. These important manuscripts shed light on the state of the Hebrew text as it was developing in the last centuries B.C. and the first century A.D.

Sept.   Septuagint (meaning 'seventy'); often abbreviated as the Roman numeral (LXX), the name given to the main Greek version of the Old Testament. According to tradition, the Pentateuch was translated in Egypt in the third century B.C. by 70 (or 72) translators, six from each tribe, but the precise nature of its origin and development is not fully known. It was intended to provide Greek-speaking Jews with a convenient translation. Subsequently it came to be much revered by the Christian community.

Symm.   Symmachus, another Greek translator of the Old Testament (beginning of the third century A.D.), who tried to combine literalness with good style. Both Lucian and Jerome viewed his version with favour.

Targ.   Targum, a name given to various Aramaic versions of the Old Testament, produced over a long period and eventually standardized, for the use of Aramaic-speaking Jews.

Theod.   Theodotion, the author of a revision of the Septuagint (probably second century A.D.), very dependent on the Hebrew text.

Vulg.   Vulgate, the most important Latin version of the Old Testament, produced by Jerome about A.D. 400, and the text most used throughout the Middle Ages in western Christianity.

[. . .]   In the text itself square brackets are used to indicate probably late additions to the Hebrew text.

(Fuller discussion of a number of these points may be found in *The Making of the Old Testament* in this series.)

TABLE OF EVENTS IN THE SEVENTH AND SIXTH CENTURIES B.C. BEARING ON THE BOOK OF JEREMIAH

Judah		Egypt	Babylon
Manasseh 687–642 Amon 642–640 Josiah 640–609	Death of Assurbanipal of Assyria about 630 Call of Jeremiah to be a prophet 627 Josiah's reformation based upon the book of Deuteronomy 621 Fall of Nineveh 612 Battle of Megiddo and Josiah's death 609	Psammetichus I 664–610 Necho II 610–594	Nabopolassar 626–605
Jehoahaz (Shallum) 609 Jehoiakim 609–598	Egypt defeated by Nebuchadrezzar at Carchemish 605		Nebuchadrezzar 605–562
Jehoiachin 598–597	Capture of Jerusalem by Nebuchadrezzar and the deportation of Jehoiachin and other leading citizens into exile in Babylon 597		
Zedekiah 597–587	Fall of Jerusalem to Nebuchadrezzar and a second and more extensive deportation of Judaeans to Babylon 587. Judah henceforth organized as a province of Babylonian empire	Psammetichus II 594–589 Hophra 589–570	
Gedaliah (governor) 587–?	Jeremiah taken into exile in Egypt soon after assassination of Gedaliah Jehoiachin released by Amel-Marduk (Evil-merodach) from prison in Babylon 562	Amasis 570–526	Amel-Marduk (Evil-merodach) 562–560 Neriglissar 560–556 Labashi-Marduk 556 Nabonidus 556–539 Babylon conquered by Cyrus (550–530), King of Persia. End of exile 539

THE BOOK OF THE PROPHET

JEREMIAH

✳ ✳ ✳ ✳ ✳ ✳ ✳ ✳ ✳ ✳ ✳ ✳ ✳

JEREMIAH'S MINISTRY IN ITS HISTORICAL
SETTING

Jeremiah received his call to be a prophet in the thirteenth year of the reign of Josiah king of Judah (640–609 B.C.; see 1: 2), that is, in 627 B.C. His ministry took place during the period from this year until not long after 587 B.C. when a group of Judaeans, fearing reprisals by the Babylonians because of the assassination of Gedaliah whom Nebuchadrezzar had appointed governor of Judah after the destruction of Jerusalem, forced Jeremiah to accompany them into exile in Egypt (cp. 43: 1–7). The last recorded episode of his career took place there and it was there, we must presume, that he eventually died. He came from Anathoth, about 3 miles (about 4·8 km) north of Jerusalem, and was the son of a priest, Hilkiah, though there is nothing to suggest that Jeremiah himself was a priest. Jeremiah's prophetic ministry spanned a period of over forty years and covered the reigns of the last five kings of Judah. These years, though they began with renewed hopes under Josiah, saw the decline and fall of Judah and the destruction of Jerusalem at the hands of the Babylonians under Nebuchadrezzar, the ablest monarch of the neo-Babylonian empire which emerged and rose to power towards the end of the seventh century B.C.

Josiah was the grandson of Manasseh whose long reign (687–642 B.C.), according to the author of 2 Kings 21, saw a resurgence of Canaanite and other pagan cults which his father Hezekiah had suppressed by a reformation carried out towards the end of the eighth century B.C. (2 Kings 18: 3ff.).

Manasseh is portrayed in 2 Kings 21 as a patron and innovator of pagan cults and practices on a scale hitherto unsurpassed in Judah. His son and immediate successor Amon (642–640 B.C.), about whom we know very little, was assassinated by a group of his courtiers. His assassins were themselves executed by a popular rising among the people, who placed his son Josiah on the throne.

Josiah proved himself to be a courageous leader of the nation. He gained independence for his kingdom from the Assyrians who had held Palestine and neighbouring lands in subjection for more than a century. We cannot be certain when Josiah made his first move to shake off the Assyrian yoke. The last years of the reign of the Assyrian king Assur-banipal, who died shortly before or shortly after 630 B.C., were troubled ones for the Assyrians, largely because of internal struggles, and it is possible that Josiah took advantage of this to make his move for national independence. But though independence was achieved, the struggle to maintain it went on and we know that Josiah was killed in battle at Megiddo against the Egyptians in 609 B.C. when he was attempting to prevent them from getting across to help the Assyrians against the Babylonians whose rise to a position of power and control of the Near East was beginning at that time.

What Josiah is most remembered for in the Old Testament, however, is the reformation he carried out on the basis of 'the book of the law' found in the temple in the eighteenth year of his reign (622 B.C.; 2 Kings 22: 1 – 23: 25; cp. 2 Chron. 34 which presents a different account, strikingly divergent in a number of ways from that in 2 Kings, but which, if used with caution, provides some supplementary information to that given in 2 Kings). Scholars are almost unanimously agreed that 'the book of the law' was the book of Deuteronomy with the exception of a few chapters, for the reforms carried out by Josiah, especially his centralization of worship in Jerusalem, reflect closely the main demands of Deuteronomy. The information supplied by the narrative in 2 Kings 22: 1 – 23: 25

together with a study of Deuteronomy itself has revealed that this book was composed probably during the second half of the seventh century B.C., though a few chapters (most of chs. 1–4 and 29–34) are generally agreed to have been added some time later, very probably during the period of the exile.

Deuteronomy was the product of a group of reformers who sought to renew the nation's loyalty to its God, Yahweh, and to extirpate the Canaanite religion and cults which had gained widespread popularity among the people and threatened to submerge Yahwism altogether. In a preaching style striking for its intensity and sense of urgency they emphasized God's love for his people, his redemption of them from bondage in Egypt and his gracious gift to them of the good land of Canaan, all of which was intended to evoke a response of love and fidelity from Israel, God's chosen people. The book is imbued with warnings against the danger of apostasy, of worshipping other gods, and laws are set forth to deal with any attempt to encourage such worship. The abolition of all sanctuaries apart from 'the place' appointed by God for the nation's cult is demanded. (Various considerations make it clear that 'the place' is to be identified with Jerusalem.) The nation is described as under an oath of obedience to the divine will, the law as set forth in the central section of the book (chs. 12–26). Promises of blessing as reward for faithfulness are set forth but also threats of the dire consequences of apostasy and disobedience (ch. 28). (For fuller detail, see *Deuteronomy* in this series.)

We know almost nothing of Jeremiah's life during the reign of Josiah and can only infer what the content of his message was during those years. For although there are many narratives in the book describing incidents and events in his life during the reigns of Jehoiakim and Zedekiah, there is none dealing with the period of Josiah's reign. Furthermore only one short passage in the book is explicitly dated in the reign of Josiah (3 : 6–11) and it is almost certainly not from Jeremiah but was composed by the Deuteronomic authors to whom the book owes its present form (see the discussion of the composition of

3

the book on pp. 10–16). The evidence suggests that the most intense period of Jeremiah's ministry took place during the reigns of Jehoiakim and Zedekiah. This is not surprising, for the period during which these two kings reigned contrasted sharply with the years of revival, reformation and hope under Josiah. We note also that in 605/4 B.C. Jeremiah made a collection of the oracles which he had hitherto spoken and now applied them anew to the situation at this time under Jehoiakim (see ch. 36). This also points to the new and intensified activity of the prophet which began with the advent of Jehoiakim to the throne.

Although we cannot be certain, it is possible that some of the sayings in, for example, chs. 2 and 3 of the book derive from the earliest years of Jeremiah's ministry. The bitter attack here on the nation's 'harlotry', its worship of the Canaanite god Baal, would certainly fit the period immediately after his call in 627 B.C. when as yet Josiah's reformation was not inaugurated (or was only in its initial stages) and the apostasy which had flourished under Manasseh would very probably still have been widespread. In addition, some of the sayings in these chapters, especially those which portray Israel as the unfaithful 'bride' of Yahweh, may be evidence of the influence on the young Jeremiah of the preaching of the great eighth-century prophet Hosea. Likewise, the impassioned appeal to the nation to turn again to God in passages such as 3: 12f., 19–22; 4: 1–9 would also fit the early years of the prophet's ministry. The evidence suggests that as time went on, and especially during the reigns of Jehoiakim and Zedekiah, Jeremiah became increasingly convinced that the nation's rebellion against God was so deep-seated that judgement was inevitable and that only through judgement could a new beginning be made. A number of commentators believe that the sayings in the early chapters of the book announcing the coming of the 'foe from the north' derive from the earliest years of Jeremiah's ministry and some have suggested that the foe in question at this stage in his preaching was the Scythians, a name used rather loosely

4

for marauding bands known from this period. But the book as it now stands clearly identifies the 'foe from the north' with the Babylonians; accordingly, it seems more likely that the oracles announcing the terrifying approach of the 'foe from the north' belong to the later stages of the prophet's ministry. They fit the early years of Jehoiakim's reign well.

What Jeremiah's attitude was towards Josiah's reformation can only be inferred. The one passage in the book (11: 1–17) which would indicate that he enthusiastically supported the reformation is very probably not from Jeremiah but from the Deuteronomic editors of the book (see the commentary on this passage on pp. 107 ff.). What we can say, however, is that Jeremiah held Josiah in the highest esteem (see 22: 15f.) and this, coupled with the aims and intentions of the reformation, which the prophet could only have welcomed, points to the strong probability that he shared the hopes to which Josiah's reforming zeal gave rise. Indeed it is possible that as a result of the reformation he withdrew from his ministry for some years. This would account for the absence of any information about his activity during Josiah's reign and for the difficulty in assigning more than a few oracles and sayings to that period. It is true that in time Jeremiah seems to have become disenchanted with the reformation. But this was not because he believed it to have been in any way wrong or even deficient in the first instance but evidently because in some circles the law which had been the foundation of the reformation became the basis for a new orthodoxy which resulted in an easy complacency and blinded the nation to the ever new and challenging word of God. In this way the law was being reduced to nothing more than a fetish (see the commentary on 8: 8–9).

As we have seen, Josiah was tragically killed at Megiddo in 609 B.C. He was succeeded by his son Jehoahaz (Shallum) who was acclaimed king by the people. But he reigned for only three months before being deposed by Pharaoh Necho, the -victor at Megiddo, who placed another son of Josiah, Eliakim (whose name as king was Jehoiakim), on the throne (cp. 22: 10–12). Under Jehoiakim (609–598 B.C.) Judah remained subject to Egypt until 605 B.C. The Egyptians exacted a heavy tribute from Judah and as if this was not a heavy enough economic burden on the nation, Jehoiakim himself, probably early in his reign, set about building a new and grandiose palace for himself for which he incurred a scathing condemnation from Jeremiah (see 22: 13–17). Jehoiakim turned out to be the very opposite of all his father Josiah had been. Not only was he a tyrant, but under him the reforms enacted by his father lapsed. He was Jeremiah's bitterest enemy. We know that he executed a prophet, one Uriah, whose message is said to have been similar to Jeremiah's, and that but for the protection afforded Jeremiah by certain state officials he too would have been removed from the scene by Jehoiakim (26: 20–4; cp. 36: 19, 26).

It is recorded in 26: 1 that at the beginning of Jehoiakim's reign Jeremiah preached his famous temple sermon in which he condemned as false the popular belief that the mere presence of the temple in Jerusalem was a guarantee against divine judgement upon the nation for its rebellion against God. (This sermon was subsequently edited and developed by the Deuteronomic editors of the book and is now found in 7: 1–15.) This in itself is evidence that Josiah's reformation had now ceased to be effective. In addition, pagan practices of the most heinous nature, the Molech cult, the chief characteristic of which was human sacrifice, again became popular (cp. 7: 31f.) as also did the cult of 'the queen of heaven' (cp. 7: 18).

As a result of all this and the disastrous policies which Jehoiakim pursued, Jeremiah's ministry now entered its most vigorous period. He became the unrelenting opponent of the king and proclaimed the inevitable judgement of God upon the nation. Very probably it was during these early years of Jehoiakim's reign that the oracles announcing the devastation to be wrought upon the country by the 'foe from the north' were proclaimed by the prophet.

For a few years the Babylonians were not an immediate threat to Judah. But this state of affairs was soon to be drastically altered. In 605 B.C. Nebuchadrezzar defeated the Egyptians at Carchemish on the Euphrates and was poised to invade Palestine itself. It was probably these events which prompted Jeremiah to compile a scroll of the oracles which he had hitherto uttered and have them re-proclaimed as a unit in the temple by his scribe Baruch (cp. ch. 36). If up to that point his oracles of judgement had been ignored or dismissed as false, in the new situation which had now come about, they took on a frightening significance for the people whose confidence was now severely shaken: the 'foe from the north' had terrifyingly materialized!

The danger which loomed for the nation at this time was overcome when, in 604 B.C., Jehoiakim submitted to the Babylonians. But his loyalty to Nebuchadrezzar was short-lived and as a result of further war between the Babylonians and the Egyptians in 601 B.C. he rebelled against his overlord. It was not for some time that Nebuchadrezzar was able to march in power to quash Judah's rebellion, though he engaged some Aramaean, Moabite and Ammonite contingents to harass Jehoiakim in the meantime (cp. 2 Kings 24: 2). Late in 598 B.C., however, the Babylonian army invaded Judah and besieged Jerusalem, Jehoiakim died (he may have been assassinated), and his eighteen-year-old son, Jehoiachin, succeeded him. When, however, only three months later, that is, in 597 B.C., Jerusalem fell to the Babylonians, the young king and his mother as well as various officials and other top-ranking citizens were carried into exile in Babylon (cp. Jer. 13: 18; 22: 24–7). Jehoiachin's uncle Mattaniah, whose throne-name was Zedekiah, became king and was to be the last reigning monarch of Judah.

Under Zedekiah the nation's decline continued. He appears to have been a weak ruler easily manipulated by his nobles. His position was not helped by the fact that Jehoiachin, though in exile, appears to have been regarded officially by the Babylonians as still being king of Judah. The exiles themselves regarded him as king, whilst in Judah itself it was popularly believed that Jehoiachin and the exiles would soon be brought back to Jerusalem (28: 1–4). Such a state of affairs would have placed limitations on Zedekiah's authority.

Jeremiah inveighed against the optimistic beliefs which sprang up after 597 B.C. that God was about to destroy the power of Babylon and return the exiles to the homeland. He announced that the yoke of Babylon would remain upon the neck of not only Judah but the other kingdoms of Syria-Palestine (ch. 28). At the same time he declared that God's blessing was already upon those in exile and that the future restoration of the nation would be brought about by God through these exiles (ch. 24), whilst those who had remained in the homeland were under divine judgement soon to befall them. He wrote to the exiles in Babylon encouraging them to settle down and assuring them of God's care for them and their ultimate redemption from bondage (ch. 29).

Because of this he became increasingly the object of abuse at the hands of his fellow countrymen and more than once during the reign of Zedekiah, and especially during the final years of it, he suffered greatly and at times came near to losing his life (cp. 20: 1f.; 37; 38). He was regarded as a traitor and was condemned and isolated. Though we canot date precisely those passionate and intensely personal outbursts of Jeremiah commonly referred to as his 'confessions' (cp. 11: 18 – 12: 6; 15: 10–18; 17: 14–18; 18: 19–23; 20: 7–13, 14–18), it is in every way probable that they belong at least for the most part to this period of his ministry.

Notwithstanding the assault on Judah and Jerusalem by the Babylonians in 598–597 B.C. and its dire consequences, the spirit of rebellion continued and given the opportunity would flare up into activity. Probably as a result of disturbances in Babylon in 594 B.C. (cp. 29: 21–3), Zedekiah became party to an attempted coalition between Edom, Moab and Tyre with a view to rebellion against the Babylonians and consultations between ambassadors of these states took place in Jerusalem (cp. ch. 27). But for reasons unknown to us nothing came of this attempt. Jer. 51: 59 may be an allusion to Zedekiah's desire to reassure Nebuchadrezzar of his continued loyalty.

But if the plans on this occasion came to nothing, outright rebellion was to come but a few years later. By 589 B.C. Zedekiah had committed himself irrevocably against the Babylonians. His reasons are not known to us. Undoubtedly the same nationalistic spirit which exhibited itself earlier and which was sustained by promises by popular prophets of an imminent reversal of the set-backs and exile of 597 B.C. asserted itself again. In addition, the Egyptians now as in times past entered the scene with encouragement to Zedekiah and assurances of military backing. Nebuchadrezzar did not delay to attack. Early in 588 B.C., the ninth year of Zedekiah's reign, the Babylonian army reached Jerusalem and besieged it whilst at the same time setting about reducing and gaining control of such strongholds as they had not already taken. Jerusalem had a brief respite later in the year when the promised, but in the end ineffectual, Egyptian help materialized and forced the Babylonians to lift the siege on Jerusalem (cp. 37: 3–5). But the Egyptians were quickly routed by the Babylonians who promptly surrounded Jerusalem again. Resistance continued for months. During this time and probably also before it Zedekiah considered surrendering and suing for peace. He consulted Jeremiah who had all along called for submission to Nebuchadrezzar (cp. 21: 1–7; 37: 1–10, 17f.; 38: 14–23). But in spite of the prophet's message and counsel, the resistance was carried on until 587 B.C. when the city had exhausted its food supplies (cp. 2 Kings 25: 2f.; Jer. 52: 5f.). Zedekiah got out of the capital by night in an attempt to escape but was captured near Jericho and brought to Nebuchadrezzar at Riblah in Syria. His sons were executed and Zedekiah himself, having witnessed their death, was blinded and taken in chains to Babylon where he died. A few weeks later Nebuzaradan, captain of Nebuchadrezzar's bodyguard, entered Jerusalem and razed it to the ground and burned down the temple. A further body of Judaeans were now deported to Babylon. Jeremiah, who had been imprisoned in the guard-house during the final stages of the siege, was now released by the Babylonians (cp. 39: 11–14; 40: 1–6).

Judah, now devastated and with the cream of its population either dead or in exile, became a province of the Babylonian empire. Nebuchadrezzar appointed Gedaliah as governor and the centre of his administration was Mizpah. How long he governed is not clear and estimates of anything from a few months to several years have been proposed. He was assassinated by one Ishmael who had the backing of the Ammonites (40: 13 – 41: 3). Fearing reprisals from the Babylonians, the community at Mizpah, though appealed to and warned by Jeremiah to remain in Judah (cp. 42: 7–22), fled to Egypt and forced the prophet to go with them. The last recorded episode of his ministry took place in Egypt and there, we may presume, he died, whether soon after his arrival or later we do not know.

THE BOOK OF JEREMIAH

The book of Jeremiah contains three kinds of literary material. Firstly, there are many poetic oracles and sayings such as we find in most other prophetic books in the Old Testament. Secondly, there are many narratives describing incidents and events in the life and times of Jeremiah. Thirdly, the book contains numerous sayings, some of them lengthy discourses or 'sermons', in prose. The poetic oracles are for the most part from Jeremiah himself, whilst the historical narratives are usually believed to be a biography of the prophet composed by the scribe Baruch. But the many prose sayings and 'sermons' pose the most difficult problem in understanding the composition of the book.

Scholars have long acknowledged that these prose sayings and 'sermons' are closely akin in both style and vocabulary to the Deuteronomic literature which comprises the books

Deuteronomy, Joshua, Judges, Samuel and Kings. So different are these prose sayings and 'sermons' not only in style and language but also in theological content from the poetic oracles that it is very unlikely that both types of material could have come from one and the same author. Some scholars have suggested that a group of disciples gathered round Jeremiah and subsequently recast, so to speak, some of his sayings in the Deuteronomic style and developed them along Deuteronomic lines. But we have no evidence that Jeremiah had such a following of disciples; he appears to have worked alone, accompanied only by his scribe and companion Baruch. More probably, therefore, these prose sayings and 'sermons' were composed by a group of Deuteronomic authors. This does not mean that the passages in question are simply Deuteronomic 'inventions'. Some of them (e.g. 11: 1–14; 17: 19–27) are probably not based on anything Jeremiah said. But most appear to be based on his original sayings. The Deuteronomic authors expanded and developed certain of his sayings and oracles and supplemented the prophet's own message so as to relate them to the needs of the nation at a time later than Jeremiah and to draw out their significance for that time. This means that the material in the book of Jeremiah spans a period considerably longer than that covered by Jeremiah's ministry. It embodies the message of Jeremiah and the oracles he uttered over the forty or so years of his ministry. But it also contains much which originated during the period of the exile when the Deuteronomic authors worked and sought to revive and renew the nation's life after the catastrophe which had befallen it in 587 B.C.

In addition to these prose sayings and speeches, however, it is also probable that the narratives in the book derive from the same Deuteronomic group from which the prose sayings and 'sermons' derive. Certainly in style and language they are very similar to the sort of narratives we find in the Deuteronomic literature, especially, say, in the book of Kings. Furthermore, the fact that not a few of these narratives in Jeremiah embody prose sayings and 'sermons', in some instances providing nothing more than a historical framework for such sayings and 'sermons', renders it all the more likely that both the narratives and the sermons come from the same authors. In addition, these narratives, far from being merely biographical, concern for the most part pressing theological issues which can be shown to be of importance in the Deuteronomic literature as well. The traditional view that Baruch composed these narratives must therefore be regarded as improbable, even though some of the information in them dealing with incidents in Jeremiah's life may have come from him.

We have already seen that the book of Deuteronomy in its original form (substantially chs. 5–26 and 28 of the present book) made its appearance in 622 B.C. The style and language of Deuteronomy are, however, also found in the books which follow it in the Hebrew Bible (Joshua, Judges, Samuel and Kings). The view now shared by most scholars is that the corpus of literature Deuteronomy to 2 Kings is one extended work composed by a group of Deuteronomic theologians and authors who, using sources from varying ages and places in Israel's history, have compiled a history of the nation from Moses to the exile.

These Deuteronomic authors lived and worked in the shadow of the catastrophe of 587 B.C. and their main purpose in composing their history of the nation was twofold. First, they sought to explain why Israel, God's chosen people, had suffered the terrible disasters which had befallen them, first in 722 B.C. when the northern kingdom was destroyed, and finally in 587 B.C. when Judah was destroyed and many deported to Babylon. Their explanation, in brief, was that Israel had persistently, and to an ever-increasing degree, disobeyed God's law, forsaking him and worshipping other gods. God had sent prophets through the centuries to succeed Moses, the first and greatest of the prophets (cp. Deut. 18: 15–19), and to exhort the nation to steadfast obedience to God's law. But the nation had stubbornly refused to listen to these prophets (cp. 2 Kings 17: 13–17). Because of this the nation incurred God's judgement. Secondly, however, although the theme of judgement is emphasized throughout the history, the Deuteronomic authors held out hope for the future of the people, now deprived of their land and living in exile. If, notwithstanding their past rebellion against God, they turned again in penitence to him, he would forgive them and restore them to their homeland and reconstitute them as his people (cp. Deut. 4: 29–31; 30: 1–10; 1 Kings 8: 46–53).

For our understanding of the prose sayings and 'sermons' as well as the narratives in the book of Jeremiah several themes or motifs in the Deuteronomic literature must be noted. First, great emphasis is placed throughout this literature on the central importance of the law in the life of the nation. Secondly, the prophets play a very important role: Moses was the first and greatest of the prophets and he was succeeded by a series of prophets to continue his work in proclaiming God's law and word to the nation. Thirdly, the Deuteronomic historians placed great emphasis on the solemn responsibility of the kings in directing and leading the nation's life as God's holy people and in seeing that the divine law was established and observed in the land. In their history of the monarchy they condemn most kings for not having lived up to this responsibility and for thus having been foremost in bringing disaster upon the nation because of its apostasy. Finally, as we have noted, the Deuteronomic historians also announced promises of hope for the nation's future beyond the judgement which had befallen it.

In commenting on the prose sayings and the narratives in the book of Jeremiah attention will be drawn to the presence of these and other Deuteronomic themes and motifs in them. In broad terms the purpose of the Deuteronomic authors and editors in developing and supplementing Jeremiah's words was, as in the Deuteronomic history itself, twofold. First, they sought to explain the catastrophe of 587 B.C.: it befell the nation because of its persistent refusal to obey the law of God or to pay heed to the word of God announced to it by the prophets, in this instance by Jeremiah. But this was not only instruction about the past; it was at the same time exhortation to those now in exile and living in the shadow of judgement to turn again in penitence and obedience to God. In this way these Deuteronomic authors and editors sought to bring about an inner renewal of the nation's relationship to God. Secondly, alongside this they further developed and supplemented Jeremiah's message of hope for the nation's future beyond judgement and they announced, like Jeremiah himself, that the revival and restoration of the nation to be brought about by God was to be effected through the exiles in Babylon.

All this means that a complicated history lies behind the book of Jeremiah, beginning with the individual oracles and sayings of Jeremiah which were recorded by the prophet in the scroll compiled by Baruch in 604 B.C. and subsequently expanded by the addition of later sayings of the prophet. We must assume that these recorded sayings of the prophet got into the hands of a group of Deuteronomic authors and editors who then arranged them further, expanded and developed a number of them to suit their own theological purposes, and composed many narratives alongside them. There thus arose a number of small groupings of material which were ultimately brought together into larger collections which were in turn united to form the book as it now stands.

The present book comprises four major collections which may be classified with regard to their separate main themes as follows:

(A) chs. 1–25, which comprise a number of smaller units of material, centre on the judgement announced against the nation.

(B) chs. 26–36 comprise oracles and sayings for the most part presented within a narrative framework. The section as a whole may be classified as a history of the word of God proclaimed by Jeremiah and rejected by the nation. The opening chapter introduces this theme, which reaches its climax in ch. 36.

(C) chs. 37–45 cover the period of the prophet's life and ministry from the siege and fall of Jerusalem in 587 B.C. down to the last episode in his ministry which took place in Egypt. They describe the suffering endured by the prophet at the hands of his fellow-countrymen and the subsequent vindication of both the prophet and the word he proclaimed (37: 1 – 40: 6). The section 40: 7 – 44: 30 centres on the history of the community left in Judah by the Babylonians after 587 B.C. and its eventual flight to Egypt. The purpose of all this is to show that the hope for the future did not lie either in the land of Judah itself or amongst those who fled to Egypt; the true 'remnant' of the nation through whom renewal was to come was the community in exile in Babylon.

(D) chs. 46–51 clearly comprise a separate section within the book and consist of oracles against foreign nations. In the Septuagint these chapters follow 25: 13 (25: 14 is omitted) and this may have been their original position. Section 25: 15–38 then stands as a concluding comment to them.

The book ends with a historical appendix (ch. 52) which is largely parallel to 2 Kings 24: 18 – 25: 30 but includes some additional information to what is contained in this narrative.

The Septuagint and the Hebrew texts of the book of Jeremiah differ, as has just been noted, in their placing of the oracles against foreign nations. But in addition to this major difference, the Septuagint has at many points a shorter form of the text. In many cases the shorter form amounts to nothing more than the absence of a word or two and often there is no difference in substance between the two texts. But in some passages there are longer sections found in the Hebrew but not in the Septuagint (e.g. 33: 14–26 where the Hebrew has a group of oracles centring mainly on God's promises to David, but the Greek has none of this material). The existence of these differing forms of the text is further illustrated by fragments of the text found among the Dead Sea Scrolls at Qumran. It appears that the book of Jeremiah existed in more than one form and whilst the shorter text of the Septuagint is easily explained in places as being due to nothing more than a scribal error or to the Greek translators, in other places it seems clear that the longer Hebrew text reflects a greater or lesser degree of development or supplementation of the original Jeremiah material. A good example of this is the material in ch. 33 already mentioned. Another example is contained in 29: 16–20 which is not found in the Septuagint. This passage is an announcement of judgement addressed to and against those left in Jerusalem and Judah after the deportation of 597 B.C. and as such it is out of place in this chapter, which records the letter sent by the prophet to the exiles in Babylon. The passage is probably, therefore, a secondary insertion into this chapter and may have been added in order to emphasize further that the future of Israel as the people of God would be brought about through the exiles in Babylon and not those who remained in Judah itself during the period of the exile (see the comments on the passage).

THE RELIGIOUS IDEAS OF THE BOOK OF JEREMIAH

Only a careful and thoughtful study of the book of Jeremiah itself can reveal fully the religious and theological riches it contains. But some of the main characteristics of its religious teaching and outlook may here be briefly noted to serve as a guide in reading the book.

First and foremost, as we might expect, the book has much to say about God and the predominant features of its teaching in this respect are as follows. Other 'gods' are mentioned, but they are dismissed as empty illusions. In other words the authors of the book were monotheists. Yahweh alone is God. He is creator and sustainer of the world. As a corollary to this and at the same time further evidence of it, the book is 'universalistic' in its teaching about God. Yahweh is Lord not only over Israel but over the other nations of the world and their destinies are in his hands. He controls history and, though men and nations may not acknowledge him as Lord, his sovereign will and purposes will be established. Yahweh is a holy and righteous God who stands in judgement upon all that is evil in the lives of men and nations. He sets his heart on 'justice and right upon the earth' (9:24) and man's true wisdom is to know and understand him and so to live in accordance with his divine will and thus manifest his holiness and righteousness. He is the God of unfailing love who summons men to respond to him in love and steadfast loyalty.

The book emphasizes the special relationship between Israel and God. Yet Israel's divine election was election not to privilege but to responsibility. Israel was chosen by this holy God to be his holy people so that the holiness and righteousness of God might be manifested in and through Israel to the world. Yet Israel had turned her back on God; she had broken the covenant. Like an unfaithful wife she had forsaken her first love and had gone after other 'lovers', the gods of the land of Canaan. Such behaviour was beyond belief. No other nation had forsaken its gods, even though they were no gods. Yet Israel had forsaken Yahweh, the 'spring of living water' (2:13). By doing so Israel had incurred judgement: she had been spurned by God and abandoned. The covenant had been terminated.

Yet the book of Jeremiah sees beyond this judgement to a new beginning in the relationship between Israel and God. Though rejected by God and cast out of her homeland, God would take her again to himself and reconstitute her as his people: 'in after time the land shall be peopled as of old...and Jacob shall be at rest once more, prosperous and unafraid' (46:26-7). Yet just at this point and alongside the promise for the future comes one of the deepest insights of the book. For it was now realized that Israel had not merely refused to love and obey God; Israel had been *unable* by her very nature to do so. Jeremiah saw the source of men's rebellion against God to spring from the natural perverseness of their hearts: 'The heart is the most deceitful of all things, desperately sick; who can fathom it?' (17: 9). He came to realize that Israel's sin was so deep-seated as to be part of her very nature: 'Can the Nubian change his skin, or the leopard its spots? And you? Can you do good, you who are schooled in evil?' (13: 23). Hence in the future renewal and revival of the nation to be brought about by God beyond judgement, God would change the hearts of the people. What is perhaps the most famous passage in the book of Jeremiah speaks of a new covenant between God and Israel, a covenant which would both supersede and surpass the former covenant now broken. God would set his law within the people and 'write it on their hearts' so that 'No longer need they teach one another to know the LORD; all of them, high and low alike, shall know me, says the LORD, for I will forgive their wrongdoing and remember their sin no more' (31: 31–4).

A further important feature of the teaching of the book of Jeremiah concerns the relationship between the individual and God. It is wrong to suppose that personal religion and piety and the responsibility of the individual to obey God's will and live in accordance with his divine laws had played no part in the religion of Israel before the time of Jeremiah. There is an abundance of evidence to prove that this was far from the case. Yet nowhere else in the Old Testament is the subtle power of sin over the individual more emphasized than in the book of Jeremiah. This is already obvious from the stress laid by the prophet on the perverseness of the human heart. It is also clear in the teaching of the new covenant passage which looks to the divine grace for the changing of men's hearts. Most of all, however, the relationship between the individual and God reached new depths from Jeremiah's own experiences during his ministry and from the inner struggle in his mind which was brought about by those experiences. His message met with little or no response from the nation. On the contrary, not only was his message rejected; he himself suffered greatly as God's spokesman to Israel. Frustrated and isolated to the point of sheer despair, he was thrown back upon the

God who had commissioned him to his prophetic ministry. The 'confessions' of Jeremiah, to which reference has already been made, give us the most vivid and poignant of pictures of the struggle that went on in the prophet's mind and the assault which his bitter experiences and the apparent success of evil mounted upon his faith. Most of all, however, these 'confessions' witness to Jeremiah's intense personal communion with God and, in revealing not merely the doubts which tormented him but the abyss of darkness which at times seems to have engulfed his mind, they speak of the triumph of faith. In this as in so many other ways the book of Jeremiah has still much to say to us today as it has to men down through the centuries.

✻   ✻   ✻   ✻   ✻   ✻   ✻   ✻   ✻   ✻   ✻   ✻   ✻

THE SUPERSCRIPTION TO THE BOOK

THE WORDS OF JEREMIAH son of Hilkiah, one of the 1 priests at Anathoth in Benjamin. The word of the 2 LORD came to him in the thirteenth year of the reign of Josiah son of Amon, king of Judah; also during the reign 3 of Jehoiakim son of Josiah, king of Judah, until the eleventh year of Zedekiah son of Josiah, king of Judah, was completed. In the fifth month the people of Jerusalem were carried away into exile.

✻ The superscription to the book is similar in form to that of several other prophetic books and states briefly the origins of the prophet and the period during which he ministered. (For the historical background to Jeremiah's life and ministry see pp. 1–10.)

1. *Jeremiah son of Hilkiah:* in the Old Testament the name *Jeremiah* is found a number of times of individuals other than the prophet himself. It is attested as early as the time of David (1 Chron. 12: 4, 10, 13) and as late as the time of Nehemiah

and Ezra (Neh. 10: 2; 12: 1, 12, 34). Two other individuals who bore the same name as the prophet are mentioned in 35: 3 and 52: 1 (= 2 Kings 24: 18). What the name means is not clear, but the two most likely suggestions are that it means either 'Yahweh loosens (the womb)' or 'Yahweh exalts'. Hilkiah was the name of the priest who found the 'book of the law' in the temple in 622 B.C. (2 Kings 22: 8) but though we cannot be certain it seems improbable that he is the *Hilkiah* here mentioned, that is, *Jeremiah*'s father. Like the name *Jeremiah* it was also evidently quite common.

one of the priests at Anathoth: the Hebrew is literally 'of the priests who were in Anathoth'. Most probably we are to understand this with reference to Hilkiah rather than Jeremiah, that is, that Jeremiah was the son of a priest but not a priest himself. At any rate there is no evidence that he ever functioned as a priest. We may note also the absence of any specifically priestly element or attitude in his oracles and message. Had he been a priest we might have expected that this would have had some degree of influence on both the style and content of his preaching. This is true of Ezekiel whose sayings frequently reveal his priestly background and origin.

Anathoth is probably short for Beth-Anathoth and means 'the house of the great Anath' the Canaanite goddess and 'sister' and 'consort' of the god Baal. The town thus acquired its name as a renowned shrine of this goddess. We know that Abiathar, the last chief priest of the priestly house of Eli, was banished to *Anathoth* by Solomon (1 Kings 2: 26) for his part in the plot to make Adonijah king after David. Probably, therefore, the priestly line of Abiathar lived at *Anathoth* and this accounts for the reference to *the priests at Anathoth* here. The name has been preserved in the name of the village Anata, 3 miles (about 4·8 km) north of Jerusalem. But this village is not the *Anathoth* of Jeremiah which is probably to be identified with the modern Ras el-Kharrubeh nearby.

2. *in the thirteenth year of the reign of Josiah son of Amon:* that is, in 627 B.C. (cp. 25: 3).

3. *until the eleventh year of Zedekiah son of Josiah, king of Judah, was completed:* that is, until the fall of *Jerusalem* in 587 B.C. Strictly speaking, however, this is not accurate, for Jeremiah was active during the years immediately after the fall of *Jerusalem*, as the narratives in 40: 7 – 44: 30 indicate. But there is no need to see the superscription as having originally prefaced an earlier 'draft' of the book which as yet contained no mention of Jeremiah's ministry after 587 B.C. In a very real sense the judgement which befell *Judah* and *Jerusalem* in that year marked the culmination and climax of his preaching. The short burst of renewed activity recorded in chs. 42–4, though important (see the commentary on these chapters in vol. 2), is more in the nature of an appendix to his ministry than a continuation of it. ✳

Jeremiah's call and two visions

T HE WORD OF THE LORD CAME TO ME: 'Before I 4, 5
formed you in the womb I knew you for my own;
before you were born I consecrated you, I appointed you
a prophet to the nations.' 'Ah! Lord GOD,' I answered, 6
'I do not know how to speak; I am only a child.' But the 7
LORD said, 'Do not call yourself a child; for you shall go
to whatever people I send you and say whatever I tell you
to say. Fear none of them, for I am with you and will keep 8
you safe.' This was the very word of the LORD. Then the 9
LORD stretched out his hand and touched my mouth, and
said to me, 'I put my words into your mouth. This day I 10
give you authority over nations and over kingdoms, to
pull down and to uproot, to destroy and to demolish, to
build and to plant.'

11   The word of the LORD came to me: 'What is it that
you see, Jeremiah?' 'An almond in early bloom',[a] I
12 answered. 'You are right,' said the LORD to me, 'for I am
13 early on the watch[b] to carry out my purpose.' The word of
the LORD came to me a second time: 'What is it that you
see?' 'A cauldron', I said, 'on a fire, fanned by the wind;
14 it is tilted away from the north.' The LORD said:

From the north disaster shall flare up
against all who live in this land;
15   for now I summon all peoples and kingdoms of the north,
says the LORD.
Their kings shall come and each shall set up his throne
before the gates of Jerusalem,
against her walls on every side,
and against all the cities of Judah.
16   I will state my case against my people
for all the wrong they have done in forsaking me,
in burning sacrifices to other gods,
worshipping the work of their own hands.
17   Brace yourself, Jeremiah;
stand up and speak to them.
Tell them everything I bid you,
do not let your spirit break at sight of them,
or I will break you before their eyes.
18   This day I make you a fortified city,
a pillar of iron, a wall of bronze,
to stand fast against the whole land,
against the kings and princes of Judah,
its priests and its people.

[a] *Heb.* shaked.   [b] *Heb.* shoked.

22

They will make war on you but shall not over- 19
come you,
for I am with you and will keep you safe.
This is the very word of the LORD.

☆ The remainder of the first chapter centres on the call of Jeremiah to be a prophet and comprises a description of the call-vision proper (verses 4–10) followed by two supplementary visions (verses 11–12 and 13–16) and finally further exhortation to Jeremiah together with a guarantee of his safety during his ministry (verses 17–19). It is probable that the visions here recorded were originally separate from each other and were later linked together by an editor. The fact that the chapter comprises both prose and poetic sections supports this. Furthermore, the description of Jeremiah's call-vision in verses 4–10, which is in prose, shows signs of having been given its present form by a Deuteronomic author (see below). Add to this the nature of the chapter as a whole as not only a record of the prophet's call but also an anticipatory interpretation or summary of his preaching and message which follows, and it further strengthens the view that an editor has assembled the material in this chapter to form an apt introduction and prologue to the book.

4–10. As already noted, these verses describe Jeremiah's call-vision proper. The Old Testament contains a number of such calls, for example, that of Isaiah (Isa. 6), of Ezekiel (Ezek. 1–3), Moses (Exod. 3–4), the boy Samuel (1 Sam. 3), and Elisha (1 Kings 19: 19–21). Two questions arise concerning the call of prophets such as Isaiah, Jeremiah and Ezekiel: first, why did these prophets experience a call and, secondly, why have their individual call-visions been recorded? As to the first of these, the answer very probably lies in the very nature of the ministry they each undertook. For what they each believed themselves to have to do was to take a stand over against the nation and to condemn its sinfulness and rebellion against God, to warn and to exhort. In other words 'they were called upon to abandon the fixed orders of religion which the majority of the people still considered valid – a tremendous step for a man of the ancient east to take – and because of it the prophets, in their new and completely unprecedented situation, were faced with the need to justify themselves both in their own and in other people's eyes' (von Rad). This also gives us an answer to the second question. In other words the call itself commissioned these prophets; it was the divine experience whereby they themselves were convicted of their solemn mission. At the same time the actual description they each gave of their call was intended to justify them and the message they proclaimed in the eyes of the people to whom they addressed themselves; it was their way of presenting their credentials, so to speak, to those to whom they preached their challenging and woeful words.

5. *Before I formed you in the womb I knew you for my own; before you were born I consecrated you:* Jeremiah believed himself to have been predestined by God for the solemn vocation to which he was called. Similarly, the 'servant of the Lord' in Isa. 49: 1, 5 says that God had called him 'from birth', 'he named me from my mother's womb'. We may note also that Paul believed himself to have been set 'apart from birth' (Gal. 1: 15). *I knew you for my own:* the Hebrew is literally 'I knew you' but the verb 'to know' here as elsewhere in the Old Testament means to have an intimate relationship with a person (e.g. in Amos 3: 2 where God says to his people 'you alone have I known (N.E.B. 'For you alone have I cared') of all the nations of the world'). The N.E.B. captures the sense of it here by adding the words *for my own. a prophet to the nations:* it is possible that this is an editorial addition. At any rate it appears to presuppose the presence in the book (cp. for example chs. 27, 46–51) of much material, not all of it from Jeremiah himself, concerning nations other than Israel. Since, however, Jeremiah certainly did concern himself to some extent with other *nations*, as did also, for example, Amos (chs. 1–2), Isaiah (chs. 13–23) and Ezekiel (chs. 25–32), it

cannot be ruled out that this phrase belongs to the *prophet's* own account of his call.

6. *I do not know how to speak; I am only a child:* this recalls strikingly what Moses is recorded as having exclaimed at his call: 'O LORD, I have never been a man of ready speech...I am slow and hesitant of speech' (Exod. 4: 10). We may note that this feeling of inadequacy is paralleled by Isaiah's feeling of unworthiness for the task to which he was called (Isa. 6: 5). Note also that in all three instances God rejects their protestations and proceeds to commission them. The obvious similarity between these three call-accounts shows that they conform to a stylized pattern.

8. *Fear none of them, for I am with you and will keep you safe:* Jeremiah more than any other prophet suffered greatly at the hands of his fellow-countrymen. Yet in spite of the constant danger in which his message placed him and the frequent attempts which were made on his life, he did not die until his mission was completed. Once again it is possible that we have here an editorial expansion of the prophet's original account of his call, an extension inserted in the light of the completion of his ministry.

9. *Then the LORD stretched out his hand and touched my mouth:* the same motif, the consecration of the prophet's lips for the service of God, is also found in Isa. 6: 6–7. *I put my words into your mouth:* though the same motif is found in the account of Ezekiel's call (Ezek. 2: 9 – 3: 3), this phrase is strikingly similar to God's promise to Moses in Deut. 18: 18 concerning the prophets whom he promises to raise up as successors to Moses. It is probable that at this point (cp. also the comments on verse 10) the account of Jeremiah's call has been edited by a Deuteronomic author whose hand is so much in evidence throughout the book. Elsewhere (15: 1–4, a passage also given its present form by a Deuteronomic author) Jeremiah is regarded as standing in the succession of Moses and throughout the book is frequently portrayed as one who, like Moses, demanded Israel's obedience to God's laws (cp. especially

7: 1–15; 11: 1–8; 17: 19–27; 34: 8–22; 35 – all prose passages).
In addition the phrase in verse 7 'and say whatever I tell you
to say' reproduces almost verbatim the last part of Deut. 18: 18
which may be translated 'and he shall say whatever I tell him
to say'. Thus it appears that Jeremiah here is being portrayed
as one of the divinely appointed successors of Moses, the first
and greatest of the prophets (cp. Deut. 34: 10).

10. *This day I give you authority over nations and over kingdoms:* yet another instance of the manner in which the call as
reported in the first chapter of the book presupposes the
message of the book as a whole, this particular phrase presupposing the material later in the book concerning foreign
*nations. to pull down and to uproot, to destroy and to demolish, to
build and to plant:* the terminology here employed to describe
Jeremiah's mission centres on one of the main themes of the
book, the theme of judgement and renewal or salvation after
judgement (see especially the commentary on ch. 24). Furthermore, combinations of the words here used occur only in the
prose and never in the poetry in the book (e.g. 12: 14–17).
Here, therefore, we have further evidence that this call-
narrative has been edited as an anticipatory interpretation of
the message of the prophet as presented in the book as a whole.

11–16. The two visions recorded in these verses are of a type
found elsewhere in the prophetic literature in the Old Testament: a familiar object or occurrence becomes the basis for,
or supplies the imagery for, an oracle. In verses 11–12 an
almond tree (*shākēd*) in early bloom prompts a pun and hence
an oracle *I am early on the watch* (*shōkēd*) *to carry out my purpose*.
(For an example closely similar to this and in which also there
is a play upon a word see Amos 8: 1–3.) Verses 13–16 contain
a similar oracle, prompted this time by a *cauldron...tilted away
from the north*, which provides the imagery (there is no pun in
this instance) for the judgement which is about to come from
the north upon *Judah* and *Jerusalem*. It is important to note that
in these two oracles the first chapter of the book again antici-
pates and provides a summary of themes central to the book as

a whole. The first, verses 11–12, summarizes the theme of the inevitable fulfilment of God's divine purpose of judgement and salvation, a theme which more than any other provides the foundation of the entire book (the reader is once again referred to the commentary on ch. 24). The second oracle, verses 13–16, crystallizes yet another theme of the book, the judgement which God is to inflict upon his disobedient people at the hands of the Babylonians *from the north* (cp. e.g. 3: 12, 18). (Note that even if a foe other than the Babylonians was originally thought of in these sayings about the coming foe *from the north*, in the book as it now stands there can be no doubt that it is the Babylonians who are identified as that foe.)

17–19. The fourth and final section of the first chapter returns to the actual commissioning of the prophet. *Jeremiah* is exhorted to be steadfast and faithful in his ministry and once again his safety during the turbulent years that lie ahead is promised by God who has thus called him: *They will make war on you but shall not overcome you, for I am with you and will keep you safe*. There was indeed *war* upon him but God was faithful to his promise! ✳

Exhortations to Israel and Judah

✳ The passage 2: 1 – 6: 30 constitutes a separate section within the book. It comprises oracles and sayings, mostly in poetry but with a few passages in prose, which come from different periods in Jeremiah's ministry. The N.E.B. description of the section as a whole as *Exhortations to Israel and Judah* is not really appropriate, for although some of the material in it centres on exhortation (3: 12 – 4: 4), much more is concerned with an indictment of the nation for its rebellion and sin against God and with the judgement which is about to befall Judah and Jerusalem (2: 1 – 3: 11; 4: 5 – 6: 30). For this reason a better title would be 'Israel's guilt and punishment'. ✳

27

GOD'S CHARGES AGAINST HIS PEOPLE

✶ Ch. 2 comprises five passages which were originally
independent of each other. Verses 1–3 and 14–19, which in
Hebrew address Israel in the second person singular, originally
formed one speech of the prophet into which has been inserted
another contained in verses 4–13, which addresses the nation
in the second person plural. A third unit is contained in verses
20–8 and a fourth, in which again the second person plural
form of address is employed, is contained in verses 29–32.
A fifth unit is contained in verses 33–7, in which the second
person singular form of address is again used. In 3: 1–5 the
indictment of the nation already contained in ch. 2 continues
and compares Israel's behaviour with that of an unfaithful wife,
a 'harlot with many lovers'. The passage 3: 6–11 is composed
in the characteristic prose style of the book and derives from a
Deuteronomic author. It continues the theme of the nation's
harlotry and states Judah's apostasy to be even more heinous
than that of the northern kingdom, Israel, long since destroyed and swept into exile.

These originally separate units have been combined to form
a speech in which God as 'plaintiff' accuses and indicts his
people of their rebellion against him. Thus, as we shall see, the
terminology of a lawsuit is employed: the offences of the
accused are stated and his guilt laid bare, the accused's pleas of
innocence are rejected and, just as counsel for the prosecution
in a court case might do, other possible lines of defence on the
part of the accused are anticipated and swept aside as in-
admissible. ✶

THE FAITHFULNESS OF ISRAEL'S YOUTH

2 1, 2 THE WORD OF THE LORD CAME TO ME: Go, make
a proclamation that all Jerusalem shall hear: These are
the words of the LORD:

I remember the unfailing devotion of your youth,
    the love of your bridal days,
when you followed me in the wilderness,
    through a land unsown.
Israel then was holy to the LORD,   3
        the firstfruits of his harvest;
no one who devoured her went unpunished,
evil always overtook them.
    This is the very word of the LORD.

* Israel's initial faithfulness to God is recalled, her 'unfailing devotion' of the period of the wandering in the wilderness and before the settlement in Canaan after which she became increasingly involved in the worship of Canaanite gods. At the same time God's love and devotion for his 'bride' Israel is emphasized, his election of Israel and the protection he gave her from all who attacked or threatened her. The recollection of this 'honeymoon' period serves to heighten further the nation's subsequent apostasy.

2. *unfailing devotion:* this translates the Hebrew *ḥesed*, one of the richest words in the Old Testament, used to describe the qualities of loyalty, steadfastness, unswerving love and faithfulness. It is a favourite word of Hosea who employs it to summarize God's demand of his people (cp. Hos. 6: 6). The description of the period before the settlement in Canaan as a time when Israel was faithful to God is also found in Hosea. These points of contact between Jeremiah and Hosea together with others still to be noted probably indicate that Jeremiah was influenced by the preaching of his predecessor.

3. *holy:* the basic concept here is Israel's 'separateness' from other peoples. *the firstfruits of his harvest* further emphasizes this, for just as *the firstfruits* of *harvest* and flock were to be dedicated to God and not used for ordinary requirements, so also Israel as God's *firstfruits* was dedicated to him so that

anyone who sought to 'devour' her stood under judgement in the same way as the 'profane' use of *the firstfruits* was forbidden and would incur divine judgement. ✻

APOSTASY

4 Listen to the word of the LORD, people of Jacob, families
5 of Israel, one and all. These are the words of the LORD:

> What fault did your forefathers find in me,
>> that they wandered far from me,
> pursuing empty phantoms and themselves becoming
>> empty;
6 that they did not ask, 'Where is the LORD,
>> who brought us up from Egypt,
>> and led us through the wilderness,
>> through a country of deserts and shifting sands,
>> a country barren and ill-omened, where no man
>>> ever trod,
>> no man made his home?'
7 I brought you into a fruitful land
>> to enjoy its fruit and the goodness of it;
>> but when you entered upon it you defiled it
>> and made the home I gave you loathsome.
8 The priests no longer asked, 'Where is the LORD?'
> Those who handled the law had no thought of me,
>> the shepherds of the people rebelled against me;
>> the prophets prophesied in the name of Baal
>> and followed gods powerless to help.
9 Therefore I will bring a charge against you once more,
>> says the LORD,
>> against you and against your descendants.

30

Cross to the coasts and islands of Kittim and see,   10
send to Kedar and consider well,
see whether there has been anything like this:
has a nation ever changed its gods,   11
   although they were no gods?
But my people have exchanged their Glory
   for a god altogether powerless.
Stand aghast at this, you heavens,   12
   tremble in utter despair,
      says the LORD.
Two sins have my people committed: 13
   they have forsaken me,
   a spring of living water,
and they have hewn out for themselves cisterns,
cracked cisterns that can hold no water.

✻ After the 'honeymoon' period Israel forsook God to worship other gods and for her apostasy she now stands accused by God who as plaintiff brings 'a charge' against her (verse 9). Such apostasy defies explanation! It cannot be God's 'fault' (verse 5). On the contrary, it was he to whom Israel owed its redemption from bondage in Egypt and the gift of the good land (verses 6–7). Such apostasy is also incredible (verses 10–11), for in electing and redeeming Israel Yahweh showed himself to be God indeed, yet Israel forsook him to follow 'gods powerless to help' (verse 8), nothing but 'empty phantoms' (verse 5). Even the heathen do not forsake their gods as Israel has forsaken her God (verses 10–11).

4. *people of Jacob*: synonymous with *Israel*, the patriarch *Jacob* having been renamed *Israel* as the father of the twelve tribes of Israel (cp. Gen. 32: 28).

5. *What fault did your forefathers find in me?*: the question is rhetorical, the obvious answer 'none' being implied in the very description of what God had done for his people. *pursuing*

31

empty phantoms and themselves becoming empty: the translation attempts to represent a pun in the Hebrew text itself.

6–7. These verses summarize Israel's salvation history, briefly relating the deliverance *from Egypt,* God's gracious protection of his people during their journey through *the wilderness* and his gift to them of the good *land* of Canaan, all of which supplies the answer to the question posed in verse 5. Yet in spite of all God had wrought on her behalf, Israel soon abandoned him, choosing instead to worship other gods and so defiling the very land which he had given her.

8. *The priests no longer asked, 'Where is the LORD?':* the temporal and spiritual leaders of the nation are condemned for having led the people astray. *The priests* head the list as those whose office it was to guide and lead the nation's worship of God but who instead cultivated and encouraged the cults of other gods at Israel's sanctuaries.

Those who handled the law had no thought of me: those (probably also *priests*) whose responsibility it was to instruct the nation in God's *law* were themselves ignorant of it; they did not 'know' God (the Hebrew text is literally 'those who handled the law did not know me'). To 'know' God meant to acknowledge the claims he had to Israel's love and obedience and to respond to these claims with the whole of one's being. Hosea also condemned the nation as being without 'knowledge of God' (Hos. 4: 1, 6; cp. in vol. 2 the comments on 31: 34). *the shepherds of the people rebelled against me:* a reference to the nation's rulers; 'shepherd' is often used in this sense, both in the Old Testament (e.g. Ezek. 34) and in the ancient Near East generally. *the prophets prophesied in the name of Baal:* though El was the head of the Canaanite pantheon, it was *Baal* the storm-god and giver of fertility who was mainly worshipped and whose cult more than any other was a constant threat to the worship of Israel's God Yahweh. Another name in the Old Testament for this god is Hadad.

9. *Therefore I will bring a charge against you: charge* is a translation of the ordinary word for 'lawsuit' in Hebrew.

10. *Cross to the coasts and islands of Kittim and see, send to Kedar and consider well: Kittim* is the Hebrew name for Cyprus and by extension, as here, for the islands and peoples in the Mediterranean west of Palestine. *Kedar* designates an Arabian tribe to the east. Hence the statement means that whether one goes to the west or the east one will not find a people who have forsaken their gods (even though in reality they are no gods!). But irony of ironies! Israel has forsaken her God, who is God indeed and has proved himself to be such, to worship the 'no gods' such as these nations in their ignorance worship.

12. *Stand aghast at this, you heavens:* the *heavens*, which here epitomize God's created order and conform perfectly to his divine will, are summoned to witness the unbelievable behaviour of Israel in rebelling against him and his will. Such behaviour is the very antithesis of rational behaviour and common sense (cp. also Isa. 1 : 2).

13. *cracked cisterns that can hold no water: cisterns* were widely used in Palestine to hold *water*, especially for use during the long, hot and dry summer. The porous limestone rock of Palestine had to be lined with plaster to make the *cisterns* watertight. A cistern whose lining was *cracked* was thus useless. So also, Jeremiah announces, are the 'gods' in which Israel has foolishly put her trust: they are as useless as a *cracked* cistern which will *hold no water* and thus, when need arises, will prove disastrous for all who rely on them. Israel's action is all the more incredible, since God was *a spring of living* (i.e. running) *water*, a security vastly superior to the use of *cisterns*, which it renders unnecessary. *

THE CONSEQUENCES OF APOSTASY

Is Israel a slave? Was he born in slavery?   14
If not, why has he been despoiled?
Why do lions roar and growl at him?   15
Why has his land been laid waste,

why are his cities razed to the ground[a] and abandoned?

16   Men of Noph and Tahpanhes
       will break your heads.

17   Is it not your desertion of the LORD your God
       that brings all this upon you?[b]

18   And now, why should you make off to Egypt
       to drink the waters of the Shihor?
       Or why make off to Assyria
       to drink the waters of the River?

19   It is your own wickedness that will punish you,
       your own apostasy that will condemn you.
       See for yourselves how bitter a thing it is and how
          evil,
       to forsake the LORD your God and revere me no
          longer.
       This is the very word of the Lord GOD of Hosts.

✱ What a reversal of Israel's fortunes! Although at one time
God's holy and protected people whom no enemy attacked
with impunity (cp. verse 3 which, as already noted, was
originally probably followed immediately by verses 14–19),
the nation has been despoiled at the hands of foreign nations.
The explanation of this is not that Israel had been 'a slave' or
one 'born in slavery' (verse 14) but that the nation had brought
disaster upon itself through its rebellion against God (verse 17).
Nor would political alliances save the nation (verse 18); its
apostasy would bring inevitable judgement upon it (verse 19).

16. *Noph:* the Hebrew name for Memphis, the ancient
Egyptian city situated about 13 miles (nearly 21 km) south of
modern Cairo. *Tahpanhes* is probably to be identified with
modern Tell Defneh near lake Menzaleh in northern Egypt.

[a] razed to the ground: *so some MSS.; others* burnt.
[b] *So Sept.; Heb. adds* at the time of one who leads you on the way.

18. The historical background to this verse is problematic. It appears to refer to the involvement of Judah in an alliance with *Egypt* and *Assyria*, presumably against the Babylonians. Such an alliance cannot have taken place before 609 B.C., for in that year Josiah had been killed in an attempt to frustrate Egyptian help reaching the Assyrians who, in spite of their defeat in 612 B.C., were evidently still harassing the Babylonians. Most likely, therefore, the background to such an alliance is the early part of Jehoiakim's reign after 609 B.C. He was subject to *Egypt* from 609 to 605 B.C. (cp. 2 Kings 23: 34f.) and we may see here a reference to his co-operation with *Egypt* and what remained of the Assyrian forces against the Babylonians. *Egypt* was defeated at Carchemish in 605 B.C. and thereafter Judah became subject to the Babylonians. *Shihor:* perhaps a tributary of the Nile or one of the lakes east of the Nile delta. It is here employed evidently as another way of referring to the Nile. *the River* is the Euphrates. ✻

FURTHER CHARGES AGAINST ISRAEL

Ages ago you broke your yoke and snapped your traces,   20
    crying, 'I will not be your slave';
    and you sprawled in promiscuous vice
    on all the hill-tops, under every spreading tree.
I planted you as a choice red vine,   21
    true stock all of you,
yet now you are turned into a vine
    debased and worthless !
The stain of your sin is still there and I see it,   22
though you wash with soda and do not stint the
       soap.
    This is the very word of the Lord GOD.
How can you say, 'I am not polluted, not I !   23
    I have not followed the Baalim'?

35

Look how you conducted yourself in the valley;
    remember what you have done.
    You have been like a she-camel,
twisting and turning as she runs,
24   rushing alone into[a] the wilderness,
snuffing the wind in her lust;
    who can restrain her in her heat?
No one need tire himself out in pursuit of her;
    she is easily found at mating time.
25 Why not save your feet from stony ground
    and your throats from thirst?
But you said, 'No; I am desperate.
    I love foreign gods and I must go after them.'
26 As a thief is ashamed when he is found out,
    so the people of Israel feel ashamed,
they, their kings, their princes,
    their priests and their prophets;
27 they say 'You are our father' to a block of wood
    and cry 'Mother' to a stone.
But on me they have turned their backs
    and averted their faces from me.
And now on the day of disaster they say,
    'Rise up and save us.'
28 Where are they, those gods you made for yourselves?
Let them come and save you in the day of disaster.
For you, Judah, have as many gods as you have towns.[b]

✣ God's indictment of the nation continues and her apostasy
is described in varying metaphors.

[a] rushing alone into: *prob. rdg.; Heb.* a wild-ass taught in.
[b] towns: *or* blood-spattered altars.

36

20. *you broke your yoke and snapped your traces:* Israel's desertion of God is compared to an animal which has broken its
yoke and *traces* and has escaped from its master and owner. In
the second half of the verse Israel is likened to a harlot, *on all
the hill-tops, under every spreading tree* being a reference to her
worship of Baal at Canaanite shrines or 'high-places'. Since
the cult of Baal centred on fertility rites involving sexual acts,
the description of Israel's worship of Baal as harlotry is all the
more apt (cp. also Hos. 2).

21. *I planted you as a choice red vine:* with this verse we may
compare the 'Song of the Vineyard' in Isa. 5, where the
prophet likens Israel to a vineyard carefully prepared by its
owner and sown with *red* vines but at harvest time yielding
useless wild grapes.

23. *How can you say, 'I am not polluted, not I! I have not
followed the Baalim'?:* in a number of places in the remainder
of the chapter the accused's defence and pleas of innocence are
anticipated and rejected. Here God as both plaintiff and counsel
for the prosecution, so to speak, rejects in advance any plea on
Israel's part to be innocent of worshipping Baal, pointing to the
nation's practice of human sacrifice *in the valley*, that is, the
notorious Valley of Ben-hinnom outside Jerusalem (cp.
e.g. 7: 31f.; 2 Kings 23: 10). It is from the Hebrew *ge hinnom*
'valley of Hinnom' that the word 'Gehenna' derives. By the
first century B.C. this word had come to denote the place of
fiery torment which was believed to be the punishment of the
wicked either immediately after death or after the Last
Judgement. In 2 Kings 23: 10 it is recorded that Josiah destroyed the cult in question 'so that no one might make his son
or daughter pass through the fire in honour of Molech'. From
Jeremiah's oracle here as also from other passages in the book
we must assume that the cult sprang up again in spite of
Josiah's reformation, perhaps after his death in 609 B.C. *You
have been like a she-camel* ('at mating time', verse 24): yet
another metaphor for Israel's apostasy.

25. This verse continues the metaphor of verse 24. So

37

desperate is the she-camel Israel for her lovers that not even the rough terrain and *thirst* of the wilderness can restrain her pursuit of them.

27. *they say 'You are our father' to a block of wood and cry 'Mother' to a stone:* a cynical allusion to the 'gods' whom Israel worshipped, very reminiscent of the highly sarcastic description of the worship of the god made from the stump of a tree in Isa. 44: 15ff. When disaster comes, however, such 'gods' are seen for what they are, powerless to help.

28. *towns:* the alternative translation noted in the N.E.B. footnote depends upon a word found in Ugaritic – a language akin to Hebrew once spoken in ancient Syria – which denotes a 'blood-daubed stone' (cp. also on 19: 15). *

WHY ARGUE YOUR CASE WITH ME?

29   The LORD answers,
        Why argue your case with me?
        You are rebels, every one of you.
30   In vain I struck down your sons,
            the lesson was not learnt;
        still your own sword devoured your prophets
            like a ravening lion.
31   *a*Have I shown myself inhospitable to Israel
            like some wilderness or waterless land?
        Why do my people say, 'We have broken away;
            we will never come back to thee'?
32   Will a girl forget her finery
            or a bride her ribbons?
            Yet my people have forgotten me
            over and over again.

[a] *Prob. rdg.; Heb. prefixes* You, O generation, see the word of the LORD.

How well you pick your way in search of lovers!   33
Why! even the worst of women can learn from you.
Yes, and there is blood on the corners of your robe –   34
    the life-blood of the innocent poor.
        You did not get it by housebreaking
        but by your sacrifices under every oak.
    You say, 'I am innocent;   35
    surely his anger has passed away.'
    But I will challenge your claim
        to have done no sin.
Why do you so lightly change your course?   36
Egypt will fail you as Assyria did;
    you shall go out from here,   37
        each of you with his hands above his head,
    for the LORD repudiates those in whom you trusted,
    and from them you shall gain nothing.

✻ Although they were originally probably two separate sayings, verses 29–32 and 33–7 have been combined to continue God's lawsuit against his people.

29. *Why argue your case with me?:* note once again the terminology of a law court scene. The case against Israel is open and shut: they are rebels!

30. *In vain I struck down your sons, the lesson was not learnt:* though time and again punished for her sins, Israel persisted in her apostasy, unrepentant and recalcitrant. With this we may compare Amos 4:6–11 where the prophet recalls a number of forms of punishment inflicted by God upon Israel yet without result: 'you did not come back to me'. *still your own sword devoured your prophets:* the *prophets*, sent by God to warn the nation of the consequences of its rebellion, were murdered. We recall the poignant words of Jesus about Jerusalem: 'O Jerusalem, Jerusalem, the city that murders the prophets and stones the messengers sent to her!' (Matt. 23: 37).

39

31. *Have I shown myself inhospitable to Israel?:* As with verse 5 above, the question is rhetorical, the implied answer being 'no'. Indeed more, for the question may be seen as a rhetorical device for stating the very opposite of what is asked: far from being *inhospitable to Israel like some wilderness or waterless land,* God has been the very source of life to the nation!

33. *Why! even the worst of women can learn from you:* the image employed is of a prostitute highly adept at soliciting 'lovers'. So Israel is adept at pursuing her 'lovers', the Baalim.

35. *You say,* '*I am innocent*';...*But I will challenge your claim to have done no sin:* once again we have law court terminology. Israel's plea of not guilty is rejected.

36–7. Once again, as in verse 18, alliances with foreign powers will not save the nation. Since evidently *Assyria* is no longer in any position to help and *Egypt* is the ally in question, the oracle comes from the period just before 605 B.C. when the Egyptians were routed by the Babylonians at Carchemish. It is possible, however, that the reference to *Assyria* has in mind earlier treaties between Judah and the Assyrians during the eighth century B.C. which Isaiah so vigorously condemned. ✻

ISRAEL'S HARLOTRY

3

> [a]If a man puts away his wife
>   and she leaves him,
> and if she then becomes another's,
>   may he go back to her again?
> Is not that woman[b] defiled,
>   a forbidden thing?
> You have played the harlot with many lovers;
>   can you come back to me?
>   says the LORD.

[a] *So Sept.; Heb. prefixes* Saying.
[b] *So Sept.; Heb.* land.

Look up to the high bare places and see: 2
  where have you not been ravished?
You sat by the wayside to catch lovers,
  like an Arab lurking in the desert,
and defiled the land
  with your fornication and your wickedness.
Therefore the showers were withheld   3
  and the spring rain failed.
But yours was a harlot's brow,
  and you were resolved to show no shame.
Not so long since, you called me 'Father,   4
  dear friend of my youth',
thinking, 'Will he be angry for ever?   5
  Will he rage eternally?'
This is how you spoke; you have done evil
  and gone unchallenged.

* Although an originally independent oracle, this passage has been placed here because it centres on Israel's 'harlotry' which forms one of the main themes of the preceding chapter.

1. The law underlying the statement here is contained in Deut. 24: 1–4 according to which a woman who had been divorced by her first husband and had married a second husband and was in turn divorced by him could not be remarried to her first husband for whom she had become 'unclean' through her second marriage. Such a remarriage was 'abominable to the LORD'. The point being made here is that Israel, God's *wife*, is even worse than a divorced woman who could not be remarried to her first husband: for Israel, after she had left her 'husband', God, had *played the harlot with many lovers*, thus rendering her uncleanness even more intense than a woman who had been related to only one husband after her first divorce.

Is not that woman defiled?: as noted in the N.E.B. footnote, this translation is based upon the Septuagint and suits the context. On the other hand, the Hebrew text 'Is not that land defiled' may well be correct, the statement being a further reference to the law in Deut. 24: 1–4 where the remarriage of a *woman* to her first husband is regarded as bringing 'sin upon the land' (verse 4).

2. *Look up to the high bare places:* a further reference to the Canaanite shrines where Israel had been *ravished*, that is, where she had engaged in the cult of Baal with its fertility and sexual rites. *like an Arab lurking in the desert:* the image is of an Arabian brigand taking up position *in the desert* to attack a caravan. Likewise Israel spares no effort *to catch lovers*.

3. *Therefore the showers were withheld and the spring rain failed:* the point of this is twofold. First, the rainfall, so essential for agriculture in a land as parched as Palestine during several months of the year, was *withheld* as punishment for Israel's apostasy and as an attempt to turn her again to God. We may compare with it 2: 30 (see the comment on this). But secondly, the withholding of the *rain* by God was to show Israel that he alone was the source of the fertility of the land and its produce. The thought here again is identical with that of Hosea and especially with Hos. 2. Indeed a glance at this same chapter reveals a number of striking similarities between its contents and the section of Jeremiah with which we have been concerned here (2: 1 – 3: 10): in both, the marriage metaphor is a pronounced feature (cp. also Hos. 1); Israel's 'harlotry' is emphasized, her irrepressible lust for her 'lovers' the Baalim; the Canaanite fertility cult is Israel's undoing; it is Israel's God Yahweh and not Baal who is the true source of the fertility of the land and its rich produce in field, flock and herd. These similarities very probably indicate that Jeremiah was influenced at this point of his preaching by his illustrious predecessor of the previous century.

But yours was a harlot's brow: the hard *brow* was used metaphorically, as a symbol for stubbornness (cp. Isa. 48: 4), and that is very probably what is meant here rather than, as has

sometimes been suggested, a reference to some sort of in-
signia or mark placed as a distinguishing feature on a prostitute's forehead. ✻

APOSTATE ISRAEL AND FAITHLESS JUDAH

In the reign of King Josiah, the LORD said to me, Do you 6
see what apostate Israel did? She went up to every hill-top
and under every spreading tree, and there she played the
whore. Even after she had done all this, I said to her, Come 7
back to me, but she would not. That faithless woman, her
sister Judah, saw it all; she*a* saw too that I had put apostate 8
Israel away and given her a note of divorce because she
had committed adultery. Yet that faithless woman, her
sister Judah, was not afraid; she too has gone and played
the whore. She defiled the land with her thoughtless 9
harlotry and her adulterous worship of stone and wood.
In spite of all this that faithless woman, her sister Judah, 10
has not come back to me in good faith, but only in pre-
tence. This is the very word of the LORD.

The LORD said to me, Apostate Israel is less to blame 11
than that faithless woman Judah.

✻ In the foregoing passage the nation was compared to a
woman twice divorced who is not allowed to remarry her
first husband for whom she has become unclean. As we have
seen, Israel was regarded as even more unclean than a woman
in such a position. In this next section a further comparison is
made, this time between *Judah* and the northern kingdom,
Israel, long since driven into exile because of its apostasy, and
once again the comparison is unfavourable – *Judah*'s apostasy
has outstripped even that of the northern state (verse 11), for

[a] *So one MS.; others* I.

43

notwithstanding the warning given to Judah by the fate of the
northern kingdom, she persisted in her 'whoredom'.

The passage is composed in the characteristic prose style of
the book and is probably the work of a Deuteronomic editor.
It serves the purpose of rounding off the complex of sayings
which precede it and to which it is clearly closely linked in
content, whilst at the same time forming an introduction to
the material which follows. ✻

EXHORTATIONS TO TRUE REPENTANCE

✻ Section 3: 12 – 4: 4 comprises a number of originally
separate sayings the main theme of which is exhortation to
true repentance. Because of their common theme they have
been brought together by an editor who has connected them
with the complex which precedes them (2: 1 – 3: 11), whilst
the note of warning sounded at the end of them (4: 4)
connects them with the ensuing complex of sayings in 4: 5 –
6: 30, the central theme of which is the announcement of
imminent disaster upon the nation. ✻

SUMMONS AND PROMISES

12 Go and proclaim this message to the north:

> Come back to me, apostate Israel,
>> says the LORD,
> I will no longer frown on you.
> For my love is unfailing, says the LORD,
>> I will not be angry for ever.

13 > Only you must acknowledge your wrongdoing,
> confess your rebellion against the LORD your God.
> Confess your promiscuous traffic with foreign gods
> under every spreading tree,
> confess that you have not obeyed me.
>> This is the very word of the LORD.

44

Come back to me, apostate children, says the LORD, for 14
I am patient with you, and I will take you, one from a city
and two from a clan, and bring you to Zion. There will I 15
give you shepherds after my own heart, and they shall
lead you with knowledge and understanding. In those 16
days, when you have increased and become fruitful in the
land, says the LORD, men shall speak no more of the Ark
of the Covenant of the LORD; they shall not think of it nor
remember it nor resort to it; it will be needed no more.
At that time Jerusalem shall be called the Throne of the 17
LORD. All nations shall gather in Jerusalem to honour the
LORD's name; never again shall they follow the promptings of their evil and stubborn hearts. In those days Judah 18
shall join Israel, and together they shall come from a
northern land into the land I gave their[a] fathers as their
patrimony.

* A glance at the text reveals that this section consists of two
separate units, the first composed in poetry (verses 12–13) and
the second in prose (verses 14–18). Of these the latter is almost
universally regarded as the work of an editor. It is composed
in the characteristic prose style of the book and most probably
therefore derives from a Deuteronomic author. It begins with
a call to repentance and a statement of God's enduring concern
for his people, all of which forms a parallel to the first part of
verse 12. Subsequently a series of promises are announced (see
notes below) which are readily understood as a positive statement of what is said in the second half of verse 12. Accordingly, we may see in verses 14–18 an editorial composition
prompted by the poetic oracle in verses 12–13 and intended
as an elaboration of it. Verses 12–13 are connected with what
precedes them by verse 11 and in their present context are

[a] *So Sept.; Heb.* your.

addressed to the exiles of the former northern kingdom, Israel. Since, however, elsewhere in the book in the genuine oracles of Jeremiah Israel is used of the whole nation, that is, in its original meaning, it is probable that verses 12–13 as spoken by Jeremiah addressed the nation as a whole and not just northern Israelites in exile.

12. *my love is unfailing:* this translates one word which is another form of the word translated 'unfailing devotion' (*ḥesed*) in 2: 2 (see the note on p. 29).

13. This summons to true repentance forms the framework for the complex as a whole, occurring here at the beginning and again at the end (4: 1–4).

14. *for I am patient with you:* the Hebrew word is *ba'alti* and could also be translated 'I have been a husband *or* master *or* Lord to you'. Either way it is an obvious play upon the word Baal ('lord', 'husband', 'master'). *and bring you to Zion:* the belief that *Zion* would be the centre of the nation redeemed from exile is found also in 31: 6, 12 and 50: 5. The same belief underlies the preaching of Deutero-Isaiah, an unknown prophet of the exile whose oracles have been preserved in Isa. 40–55 (cp. e.g. Isa. 52: 1–8). This belief had its basis in, and was a continuation of, the 'doctrine' of the sanctity and centrality of Zion/Jerusalem in the religion and theology of pre-exilic Judah: God had chosen *Zion* to be his sacred dwelling-place (so often in the Psalms; cp. e.g. Ps. 48).

15. *There will I give you shepherds:* a reference to the ideal rulers of the nation to be raised up by God (cp. also 23: 1–4).

16f. *men shall speak no more of the Ark of the Covenant of the LORD:* this very probably presupposes the destruction of the temple in 587 B.C. when, we must assume, *the Ark* was either destroyed or possibly taken by the Babylonians. *the Ark* had been the most sacred object in the temple and had been housed in the holy of holies. God was believed to be enthroned between the cherubim above *the Ark* (cp. 2 Kings 19: 15; Ps. 80: 1). The meaning of what is said here is to be understood in connection with verse 17: *At that time Jerusalem shall be called the Throne of the LORD.* Although *the Ark* as the throne of God's presence had been destroyed, *Jerusalem* itself would become acknowledged as *the Throne of the LORD* to which all nations would pay honour.

All nations shall gather in Jerusalem to honour the LORD's name: the motif of a pilgrimage of the *nations* to Zion is found also in Isa. 2: 2–4 (= Mic. 4: 1–3); and especially in Isa. 60. It is to be 'In days to come' (Isa. 2:2) and may thus be described as 'eschatological', i.e. 'belonging to the final age'.

18. *In those days Judah shall join Israel:* in its future beyond the judgement of exile the nation would once again be one people and the old division which arose after the death of Solomon in 922 B.C. would disappear (cp. also Hos. 1: 11; Isa. 11: 12–14; Ezek. 37: 15–20). *from a northern land:* that is, from exile in Babylon. ✳

A PENITENT RETURN TO GOD

I said, How gladly would I treat you as a son,   19
    giving you a pleasant land,
        a patrimony fairer than that of any nation!
    I said, You shall call me Father
        and never cease to follow me.
    But like a woman who is unfaithful to her lover,   20
    so you, Israel, were unfaithful to me.
        This is the very word of the LORD.
    Hark, a sound of weeping on the bare places,   21
    Israel's people pleading for mercy!
    For they have taken to crooked ways
    and ignored the LORD their God.
    Come back to me, wayward[a] sons;   22
    I will heal your apostasy.

[a] *Or* apostate.

47

O LORD, we come! We come to thee;
for thou art our God.

23   There is no help in worship on the hill-tops,
no help from clamour on the heights;
truly in the LORD our God
is Israel's only salvation.

24   From our early days
Baal, god of shame, has devoured
the fruits of our fathers' labours,
their flocks and herds, their sons and daughters.

25   Let us lie down in shame, wrapped round by our
dishonour,
for we have sinned against the LORD our God,
both we and our fathers,
from our early days till now,
and we have not obeyed the LORD our God.

4   If you will but come back, O Israel,
if you will but come back to me, says the LORD,
if you will banish your loathsome idols from my
sight,
and stray no more,

2   if you swear by the life of the LORD,
in truth, in justice and uprightness,
then shall the nations pray to be blessed like you[a]
and in you[a] shall they boast.

3   These are the words of the LORD to the men of Judah and
Jerusalem:

Break up your fallow ground,
do not sow among thorns,

[a] *Prob. rdg.; Heb.* him.

48

circumcise yourselves to the service of the LORD,   4
    circumcise your hearts,
men of Judah and dwellers in Jerusalem,
lest the fire of my fury blaze up and burn
    unquenched,
because of your evil doings.

* It is probable that 3: 19–20 belonged originally with
3: 1–5 to form one saying: both have in common the image of
Israel as a faithless wife and also picture the relationship
between God and his people as a father–son relationship.
Verses 21–5 are a unity though it is also possible, in spite of a
variation in the form of address, that 4: 1–2 also belonged to
them from the beginning. Verses 21–2 *a* are a plea to the nation
to turn again to God and verses 22 *b*–25 are a confession by the
nation of its rebellion and a pledge to return to God who is
their only source of salvation. The passage 4: 1–2 is God's
response to this, setting out the nature of true repentance;
4: 3–4, though originally probably independent of what
precedes it, is a further plea for true repentance and ends with
a warning of dire retribution if the nation does not rededicate
itself to the service of God.

22. *O LORD, we come! We come to thee:* with the confession
in verses 22 *b*–25 we may compare Hos. 6: 1–3; 14: 2–3.

23. *clamour on the heights:* a sarcastic reference to the cult of
Baal in the Canaanite high-places.

24. *Baal, god of shame:* the Hebrew word is literally 'the
shameful thing'. But elsewhere in the Old Testament the
word *Baal* is frequently replaced by or pronounced *bosheth*
'shame' (e.g. Saul's son's name is Ish*bosheth* in 2 Sam. 2: 8 but
was really Ish*baal* (or Esh*baal*) as indicated by 1 Chron. 8: 33).

4: 2. *then shall the nations pray to be blessed like you:* a promise
based upon God's ancient promise to Abraham that he would
be the source of blessing for all mankind (cp. Gen. 12: 3).

4. *circumcise your hearts:* circumcision (cutting away the fore-

49

skin of the male organ) has been widely practised by different peoples to prepare the male organ for use. Circumcision was regarded by the Israelites as a means of their dedication to the Lord. Jeremiah demands that their *hearts* be circumcised, uncovered and ready for the Lord. It is the inward attitude of the heart to God that matters more than outward displays or signs of allegiance to him (cp. 9: 26 and Deut. 10: 16). ✶

INVASION AND DESTRUCTION

✶ Section 4: 5–31 comprises a number of originally separate sayings which are for the most part highly graphic descriptions of the invasion of Judah and its imminent destruction by the foe from the north. As such it takes up the theme already sounded in 1: 13ff. The same theme predominates in chs. 5 and 6. ✶

THE ALARM

5 Tell this in Judah,
   proclaim it in Jerusalem,
  blow the trumpet throughout the land,
   sound the muster,
  give the command, Stand to ! – and let us fall back
   on the fortified cities.
6 Raise the signal – To Zion !
   make for safety, lose no time,
  for I bring disaster out of the north,
   and dire destruction.
7 A lion has come out from his lair,
   the destroyer of nations;
  he has struck his tents, he has broken camp,
   to harry your land
  and lay your cities waste and unpeopled.

Well may you put on sackcloth,   8
   beat the breast and wail,
for the anger of the LORD
   is not averted from us.
On that day, says the LORD,   9
the hearts of the king and his officers shall fail them,
priests shall be struck with horror and prophets
   dumbfounded.

And I said, O Lord GOD, thou surely didst deceive this   10
people and Jerusalem in saying, 'You shall have peace',
while the sword is at our throats.

✵ This passage consists of a poetic oracle announcing the
arrival of the foe from the north and sounding the alarm
throughout Judah. As such it forms a sort of prologue to the
ensuing material in the chapter and sounds the note of terror
and distress which is there so graphically presented. Verse 9 is
an editorial addition to verses 5–8, whilst verse 10 is a further
addition.

   5. *blow the trumpet:* the instrument here translated *trumpet*
appears to have been the chief signalling instrument in ancient
Israel. It was used for summoning the people to worship and
was sounded on some occasions during worship in the temple.
It was also used to warn of approaching danger and, as here,
sounded the alarm when invasion by an enemy took place. It
is seldom mentioned alongside musical instruments and this
seems to support the understanding of it as a signalling instrument, an instrument for making noise rather than music. *let
us fall back on the fortified cities:* during an invasion people living
in outlying villages as well as army units stationed here and
there throughout the land would take refuge in the large
fortified cities such as Jerusalem itself.

   6. *Raise the signal:* probably a banner or ensign of some sort
hoisted in a prominent place (a hill-top or tower). The

sounding of the trumpet would have accompanied this, thus providing both visual and aural warning of impending danger. *disaster out of the north:* see the comments on 1: 13ff.

9. The leadership of the nation, both temporal and spiritual, will collapse in disarray before the might of the invader.

10. *You shall have peace:* a reference to the activities of popular prophets who, addressing the nation in the name of God, had persistently assured the people that they had nothing to fear. We can imagine that such prophets based such assurances upon such long-established 'doctrines' as the inviolability of Zion as God's holy city and of the temple as his dwelling-place as well as on the belief in the everlasting covenant between God and the dynasty of David, and we need not doubt the sincerity of these prophets. It was the measure of Jeremiah's deeper understanding of the nature and purposes of Israel's God that he and prophets like him saw the inner reality of the situation to be quite other than these prophets believed. The problem of false prophecy is an important theme in the book of Jeremiah as a whole (cp. especially 14: 10–16; 23: 9–40; 27–9). ✼

DISASTER AND CHAOS

11   At that time this people and Jerusalem shall be told:

> A scorching wind from the high bare places in the
>   wilderness
>   sweeps down upon my people,
> no breeze for winnowing or for cleansing;

12   a wind too strong for these
>   will come at my bidding,
>   and now I will state my case against them.

13   Like clouds the enemy advances
>   with a whirlwind of chariots;
> his horses are swifter than eagles –
>   alas, we are overwhelmed!

O Jerusalem, wash the wrongdoing from your heart   14
　　and you may yet be saved;
how long will you cherish
　　your evil schemes?
Hark, a runner from Dan,   15
　　tidings of evil from Mount Ephraim!
Tell all this to the nations.   16
　　proclaim the doom of Jerusalem:
hordes of invaders come from a distant land,
howling against the cities of Judah.
Their pickets are closing in all round her,   17
　　because she has rebelled against me.
　　This is the very word of the LORD.
Your own ways, your own deeds   18
have brought all this upon you;
this is your punishment,
and all this comes of your rebellion.[a]
Oh, the writhing of my bowels   19
　　and the throbbing of my heart!
　　I cannot keep silence.
I hear the sound of the trumpet,
　　the sound of the battle-cry.
Crash upon crash,   20
　　the land goes down in ruin,
my tents are thrown down,
　　their coverings torn to shreds.
How long must I see the standard raised   21
　　and hear the trumpet call?
My people are fools, they know nothing of me;   22
silly children, with no understanding,

[a] your rebellion: *prob. rdg.; Heb. obscure.*

they are clever only in wrongdoing,
  and of doing right they know nothing.

23 I saw the earth, and it was without form and void;
      the heavens, and their light was gone.
24 I saw the mountains, and they reeled;
      all the hills rocked to and fro.
25 I saw, and there was no man,
      and the very birds had taken flight.
26 I saw, and the farm-land was wilderness,
      and the towns all razed to the ground,
    before the LORD in his anger.
27   These are the words of the LORD:
    The whole land shall be desolate,
      though I will not make an end of it.
28 Therefore the earth will mourn
    and the heavens above turn black.
    For I have made known my purpose;
    I will not relent or change my mind.

29 At the sound of the horsemen and archers
      the whole country[a] is in flight;
    they creep into caves, they hide[b] in thickets,
      they scramble up the crags.
    Every[c] town is forsaken,
      no one dwells there.

30 And you,[d] what are you doing?
    When you dress yourself in scarlet,
      deck yourself out with golden ornaments,

[a] *So Sept.; Heb.* city.   [b] into...hide: *so Sept.; Heb. om.*
[c] *So Sept.; Heb.* The whole.   [d] *So Sept.; Heb. adds* overwhelmed.

54

and make your eyes big with antimony,
  you are beautifying yourself to no purpose.
Your lovers spurn you
  and are out for your life.
I hear a sound as of a woman in labour,   31
  the sharp cry of one bearing her first child.
It is Zion, gasping for breath,
  clenching her fists.
Ah me! I am weary,
  weary of slaughter.

✶ The remainder of ch. 4 consists of a number of separate oracles and sayings most of which describe the disaster which is about to sweep through Judah. Both the imagery and the variation in the imagery as well as the terseness of each description of the coming disaster all combine to create an atmosphere of rapidly approaching catastrophe and make this passage as a whole one of the most evocative judgement speeches in the whole book.

11–12. The first image compares the invasion with the sirocco *wind* which blows from the east across the country. It can last from three days to as much as a fortnight, bringing temperatures sometimes as high as over 100° and creating a dry heat which is exhausting and parching for both man and beast as well as the vegetation. When this *wind* strikes, *winnowing* is impossible, for its sheer force would carry away the grain as well as the chaff.

13. Two further images drawn from the weather, the enemy's advance being likened to the unrelenting movement of *clouds* across the sky, and the approach of his *chariots*, drawn by *horses* moving more swiftly than an eagle swooping on its prey, to a rampaging *whirlwind* bringing devastation in its wake.

15–18. Word of the advancing enemy comes from *Dan*, a city in the extreme north of Israel, followed by a further

55   3-2

warning from Ephraimite territory further south and only a few miles north of *Jerusalem*.

19–21. The prophet identifies himself with the land in agony and turmoil at the advancing enemy troops and the *sound* of their war-cries as they rampage through *the land*.

23–6. These verses form the climax to this section as a whole and present vividly the return of chaos in the wake of the enemy's advance. The words *without form and void* are those used to describe the chaos before the creation in Gen. 1: 2; the disappearance of *light* from the heavens represents a reversal of the creation of *light* in Gen. 1: 3; the *mountains* and *hills*, for Israel one of the most abiding reminders of God's ancient creation of the world (cp. Ps. 46: 2; Prov. 8: 25), reel; *I saw, and there was no man* is another allusion to the chaos before creation and the creation of *man* (the Hebrew word for *man* is the same as in Gen. 1); the land tilled by *man* turns to desolation, whilst *towns* and cities, all signs of civilization and social order, disappear.

27. *though I will not make an end of it:* most commentators correctly see this as an insertion here, a sort of 'mitigating gloss', as it has been termed, intended to ease the picture of total chaos and destruction which the preceding verses present.

29. The picture of the advancing enemy and the terror it creates among the population is resumed.

30–1. The metaphor comparing Israel to a harlot is once again taken up. Now the nation's *lovers* seek to murder her. *Zion*, personified as *a woman in labour*, writhes in agony. *

THE WHOLE NATION IS GUILTY

* Ch. 5 is made up of a number of originally separate sayings, in some instances so closely woven together that it is difficult to separate them from each other. Verses 1–6 and 7–9 may have belonged together from the beginning: in the first God defies the prophet to find anyone in Jerusalem who acts justly; neither among the ordinary people nor the leaders of the nation can one be found. Accordingly the judgement announced

against the nation stands (verse 6). The guilt of the nation is further emphasized in verses 7–9 where again both cultic and social sins are referred to: because of all this God cannot forgive the nation but will take due vengeance upon such a people. Verses 10–14 stand out as a collection of originally separate sayings here loosely brought together. Verses 15–17 form an obvious unit describing the enemy God is about to bring against Israel and the fate that awaits the nation at its hands. Verse 18 is an editorial appendix to this poem, whilst verse 19 stands out clearly as an insertion by a Deuteronomic editor. There follow two further poems, the first describing Israel's stubborn rebellion against God (verses 20–5) and the second listing the oppression of the poor in the land at the hands of the wealthy (verses 26–9). Finally, verses 30–1 are a short saying condemning false prophets and the priests who act in conjunction with them – together they provide the kind of 'religious' leadership a sinful people likes to have! ✷

APOSTASIES PAST COUNTING

Go up and down the streets of Jerusalem 　　　5
　　and see for yourselves;
search her wide squares:
　　can you find any man who acts justly,
　　who seeks the truth,
that I may forgive that city?
Men may swear by the life of the LORD, 　　　2
but they only perjure themselves.
O LORD, are thine eyes not set upon the truth? 　3
Thou didst strike them down,
　　but they took no heed;
didst pierce them to the heart,
　　but they refused to learn.
They set their faces harder than flint

and refused to come back.

4   I said, 'After all, these are the poor,
         these are stupid folk,
     who do not know the way of the LORD,
         the ordinances of their God.

5   I will go to the great
         and speak with them;
     for they will know the way of the LORD,
         the ordinances of their God.'
     But they too have broken the yoke
         and snapped their traces.

6   Therefore a lion out of the scrub shall strike them
             down,
         a wolf from the plains shall ravage them;
     a leopard shall prowl about their cities
     and maul any who venture out.
     For their rebellious deeds are many,
         their apostasies past counting.

7   How can I forgive you for all this?
     Your sons have forsaken me and sworn by gods
         that are no gods.
     I gave them all they needed, yet they preferred
             adultery,
         and haunted[a] the brothels;

8   each neighs after another man's wife,
     like a well-fed and lusty stallion.

9   Shall I not punish them for this?
         the LORD asks.
     Shall I not take vengeance
         on such a people?

[a] *So some MSS.; others* and gashed themselves in.

✻ 1. In a similar instance recorded in Gen. 18: 22 ff. God promised Abraham to spare Sodom if ten righteous men could be found in it.

2. *swear by the life of the LORD:* to take an oath *by the life of the LORD* presupposed that he who swore such an oath worshipped Israel's God, Yahweh. Since, however, by their worship of other gods men revealed that they did not claim Yahweh as God, their oaths amounted to perjury. Their oaths were as empty as their alleged loyalty to, and worship of, Yahweh.

3. Cp. the comment on 2: 30 and 3: 3.

4. *the way of the LORD:* that is, the mode of life laid down by God for the right ordering of the nation's life in both worship and daily conduct. The second half of the verse with its reference to *the ordinances* of *God* is another way of saying the same thing.

6. *Therefore a lion out of the scrub shall strike them down:* lions were common in Palestine during biblical times but are believed to have died out by the early fourteenth century A.D. Like the *lion*, the *wolf* also was well known in ancient Palestine, whilst the *leopard* is known to have survived in Palestine as late as the present century. Because of their ferocity, voracity, strength, and other similar qualities, all three animals are frequently referred to figuratively in the Old Testament.

7. *and haunted the brothels:* the alternative translation noted in the N.E.B. footnote reflects a Canaanite cultic practice in which worshippers of Baal lacerated themselves. The same word as is here used is that which occurs in 1 Kings 18: 28 of the prophets of Baal who in their contest with Elijah on Mount Carmel 'as was their custom, gashed themselves'. ✻

VARIOUS SHORT SAYINGS

Go along her rows of vines and slash them,   10
  yet do not make an end of them.
Hack away her green branches,
  for they are not the LORD's.

11   Faithless are Israel and Judah,
        both faithless to me.
            This is the very word of the LORD.
12   They have denied the LORD,
        saying, 'He does not exist.
        No evil shall come upon us;
        we shall never see sword or famine.
13   The prophets will prove mere wind,
            the word not in them.'*a*

14   And so, because you talk in this way, these are the words
of the LORD the God of Hosts to me:

        I will make my words a fire in your mouth;
        and it shall burn up this people like brushwood.

✿ As already noted, these verses comprise several originally
separate short sayings here brought rather loosely together.
Verse 10 is an echo of the saying in 2: 21, whilst the reference
to Israel and Judah as faithless recalls 3: 6–11 where the same
word is used more than once. If the saying in verse 13 belongs,
as the N.E.B. has it, with what immediately precedes it, the
prophets referred to would have to be understood as prophets
like Jeremiah here brushed aside contemptuously by the people
as mere windbags. Whilst such an understanding of this verse
is possible, it is more likely that we should take it as a separate
saying not related to what precedes and as referring to the
popular prophets so frequently referred to elsewhere in the
book as having misled the nation. In contrast to these false
prophets who do not have God's word, that word is addressed
to Israel through Jeremiah in whose mouth it is to be as fire to
'burn up this people like brushwood' (verse 14).

    12. *He does not exist:* it is a mistake to understand this as a
statement of atheism. What the people are here alleged to have

[a] *So Sept.; Heb. adds* so may it be done to them.

said is that Israel's God Yahweh was of no account and could
be ignored. This at least was the attitude to God indicated by
the way they lived.

13. *mere wind:* the word here translated *wind* also means
spirit. Hence there is a play upon the word here: the false
prophets imagine they have the spirit of God but in reality have
nothing more than *wind*! Far from being 'filled with the spirit'
they are just windbags! ✳

A TERRIFYING ENEMY

I bring against you, Israel, a nation from afar,   15
an ancient people established long ago,
     says the LORD.
A people whose language you do not know,
     whose speech you will not understand;
they are all mighty warriors,   16
     their jaws are^a a grave, wide open,
to devour your harvest and your bread,   17
to devour your sons and your daughters,
to devour your flocks and your herds,
to devour your vines and your fig-trees.
They shall batter down the cities in which you
     trust,^b
     walled though they are.

But in those days, the LORD declares, I will still not 18
make an end of you. When you ask, 'Why has the LORD   19
our God done all this to us?' I shall answer, 'As you have
forsaken me and served alien gods in your own land, so
shall you serve foreigners^c in a land that is not yours.'

[a] their jaws are: *so Pesh.; Heb.* their quiver is.
[b] *Prob. rdg.; Heb. adds* with the sword.   [c] *Or* foreign gods.

✳ These verses are closely similar to Deut. 28: 49–57 and since there is so much material in the book of Jeremiah which derives from or owes its present form to Deuteronomic authors and editors it might be supposed that these verses, though composed as poetry, are also a Deuteronomic composition. It is widely recognized, however, that Deut. 28 as it now stands was composed in the period of the exile so that in this instance it is probable that Jeremiah's words here in verses 15–17 provided the basis for Deut. 28: 49–57.

15. *an ancient people established long ago:* most commentators agree that this cannot be a reference to the Scythians (see pp. 4 f.) but points almost certainly to the Babylonians.

16. *their jaws are a grave, wide open:* in view of the contents of verse 17, the reading here adopted by the N.E.B. on the basis of the Peshitta (the Syriac version of the Old Testament) is clearly preferable to the Hebrew reading 'their quiver'.

19. This verse together with 9: 12 *b*–16; 16: 10–13 and 22: 8–9 (all prose passages) are in style, form and content strikingly similar to Deut. 29: 22–8 and 1 Kings 9: 8–9 and derive from a Deuteronomic editor. There can be little doubt that they all presuppose the catastrophe of 587 B.C. and the exile. ✳

A FOOLISH AND SENSELESS PEOPLE

20   Tell this to the people of Jacob,
         proclaim it in Judah:
21   Listen, you foolish and senseless people,
         who have eyes and see nothing,
         ears and hear nothing.
22   Have you no fear of me? says the LORD;
         will you not shiver before me,
         before me, who made the shivering sand to bound
             the sea,
         a barrier it never can pass?

Its waves heave and toss but they are powerless;
roar as they may, they cannot pass.
But this people has a rebellious and defiant heart,   23
    rebels they have been and now they are clean gone.
They did not say to themselves,   24
    'Let us fear the LORD our God,
who gives us the rains of autumn
    and spring showers in their turn,
who brings us unfailingly
fixed seasons of harvest.'
But your wrongdoing has upset nature's order,   25
and your sins have kept from you her kindly gifts.

✶ Even the powers of nature obey God's command but Israel is rebellious against her creator and the one who bestows the blessings of nature upon her. Her rebellion is such that it has disturbed the very order of the creation.

22. *Its waves heave and toss but they are powerless; roar as they may, they cannot pass:* myths about creation in other ancient Near Eastern countries centred on a battle between the god and the sea personified as the chaos monster. Though there are allusions to a similar myth in the Old Testament (e.g. Job 26: 12; Ps. 89: 10; Isa. 51: 9 where the primaeval sea-monster Rahab is referred to; Pss. 74: 14; 104: 26; Isa. 27: 1 where Leviathan, yet another name for the chaos sea-monster, is mentioned), Israel used the language and content of such ancient Near Eastern myths metaphorically.

24. *the rains of autumn and spring showers:* the autumn *rains*, frequently referred to in translation as 'the former rain', comes in October, whilst the *spring showers*, 'the latter rains', come in March. The dry season is from May to the latter part of September.

25. *your sins have kept from you her kindly gifts:* cp. note on 3: 3. ✶

THE OPPRESSION OF THE POOR

26   For among my people there are wicked men,
    who lay snares like a fowler's net[a]
    and set deadly traps to catch men.

27   Their houses are full of fraud,
    as a cage is full of birds.
    They grow rich and grand,

28   bloated and rancorous;
    their thoughts[b] are all of evil,
    and they refuse to do justice,[c]
    the claims of the orphan they do not put right
    nor do they grant justice to the poor.

29   Shall I not punish them for this?
    says the LORD;
    shall I not take vengeance
    on such a people?

30   An appalling thing, an outrage,
    has appeared in this land:

31   prophets prophesy lies and priests go hand in hand
    with them,
    and my people love to have it so.
    How will you fare at the end of it all?

* Up to this point the emphasis has been on Israel's cultic
sins, that is, her worship of other gods and corresponding
rejection of her own God, Yahweh. These verses attack the
social injustice of the nation: those who get wealthy at the
expense of the poor, the failure to provide for the needs of the

[a] who...net: *prob. rdg.; Heb. unintelligible.*
[b] rancorous; their thoughts: *Heb. has these words transposed.*
[c] *Vulg. adds* for the widow.

helpless in society such as orphans. Such condemnations are a familiar feature in the prophetic literature.

26. *traps to catch men:* this may be a reference to devious means employed to enslave Israelite citizens.

28. *the claims of the orphan they do not put right:* Israel's law legislated for the rights and protection of the fatherless and the widow (cp. e.g. Exod. 22: 22; Deut. 14: 29).

30–1. Appended to this passage and forming a footnote, so to speak, to the chapter as a whole is this short saying condemning in general terms the religious leadership of the nation. The condemnation of both *priests* and *prophets* is found in a number of places throughout the book. The statement *my people love to have it so* reminds us of the similar remark made by Amos concerning the superficial worship of the *people* in his days: 'for you love to do what is proper, you men of Israel!' (Amos 4: 5). ✵

IMMINENT RUIN

✵ Ch. 6 comprises five easily recognizable units centring on Judah's sinfulness and the judgement which is about to overrun the nation. ✵

ZION'S END IS NEAR

Save yourselves, men of Benjamin,   6
    come out of Jerusalem,
blow the trumpet in Tekoa,
fire the beacon on Beth-hakkerem,
for calamity looms from the north
    and great disaster.
Zion, delightful and lovely: 2
    her end is near –
she to whom the shepherds come   3
    and bring their flocks with them.
There they pitch their tents all round her,
    each grazing his own strip of pasture.

4   Declare war solemnly against her;
         come, let us attack her at noon.
         Too late! the day declines
             and the shadows lengthen.
5   Come then, let us attack her by night
         and destroy her palaces.
6   These are the words of the LORD of Hosts:
         Cut down the trees of Jerusalem
             and raise siege-ramps against her,
         the city whose name is Licence,[a]
         oppression is rampant in her.
7   As a well keeps its water fresh,
     so she keeps her evil fresh.
         Violence and outrage echo in her streets;
         sickness and wounds stare me in the face.
8   Learn your lesson, Jerusalem,
         lest my love for you be torn from my heart,
             and I leave you desolate,
             a land where no one can live.

* In this first poem the prophet announces Jerusalem's imminent destruction and warns those who have fled to the city for refuge to leave it, for there is to be no refuge there. Like some of the sayings in ch. 4, this passage also presents a vivid description of the invader's advance through the land. Once again Jerusalem's sinfulness is stated and the saying ends with a further plea for repentance.

1. *Save yourselves, men of Benjamin:* since it is improbable that Jeremiah issued this warning to his fellow tribesmen (he himself was a Benjamite), we must understand it as having been addressed to the population of Jerusalem here considered as belonging to the territory *of Benjamin.* The city would have

[a] Licence: *so some MSS.; others* Visited.

66

been a place of refuge not only for its own inhabitants but also for people living in the surrounding territory. *Tekoa:* the home town of Amos and situated in the hill-country of Judah about 12 miles (or 19 km) south of Jerusalem. After the division of the Davidic-Solomonic state of Israel it was fortified by Rehoboam, 922–915 B.C. (cp. 2 Chron. 11: 6). The reference to *Tekoa* here probably indicates that it was still an important fortified town. It has been identified with modern Tequʻa. The summons to sound the alarm in this city in the south serves to highlight the unrelenting advance of the enemy. *Beth-hakkerem:* mentioned elsewhere only in Neh. 3: 14; its identity and location are uncertain, some identifying it with Ramet Raḥel or ʻAin Karim near Jerusalem, others placing it near Tekoa itself.

3. *she to whom the shepherds come:* the context suggests that *shepherds* here are to be understood as the enemies closing in on Jerusalem to besiege it (cp. verse 4). Some commentators emend slightly the text of verse 2 to read 'Has Zion become a beautiful meadow?', arguing that such an understanding of this verse is presupposed by verse 3.

6. *Cut down the trees of Jerusalem and raise siege-ramps against her:* the use of *trees* in the vicinity of a city for constructing siege-works against it was well known in the ancient Near East. Deut. 20: 19–20 knows of such a method but forbids the destruction of fruit-trees for the very practical reason that during a siege they can be a source of food for the troops besieging the enemy city. ✳

TOTAL JUDGEMENT UPON THE TOTALLY CORRUPT

These are the words of the LORD of Hosts: 9
    Glean[a] the remnant of Israel
        like a vine,
    pass your hand like a vintager one last time
        over the branches.

[a] *Prob. rdg., cp. Sept.; Heb.* Let them glean.

10   To whom can I address myself,
            to whom give solemn warning? Who will hear
                me?
          Their ears are uncircumcised;
            they cannot listen;
        they treat the LORD's word as a reproach;
            they show no concern with it.

11   But I am full of the anger of the LORD,
            I cannot hold it in.
          I must pour it out on the children in the street
            and on the young men in their gangs.
          Man and wife alike shall be caught in it,
            the greybeard and the very old.

12   Their houses shall be turned over to others,
          their fields and their women alike.
            For I will raise my hand, says the LORD,
          against the people of the country.

13   For all, high and low,
            are out for ill-gotten gain;
          prophets and priests are frauds,
            every one of them;

14   they dress my people's wound, but skin-deep only,
            with their saying, 'All is well.'
          All well? Nothing is well!

15   Are they ashamed when they practise their
                abominations?
            Ashamed? Not they!
          They can never be put out of countenance.
        Therefore they shall fall with a great crash,[a]

[a] with a great crash: *or* where they fall *or* among the
fallen.

and be brought to the ground on the day of my
reckoning.
The LORD has said it.

✻ The prophet is commanded to warn anyone who will
listen but can find no one who will pay attention. Accordingly,
he proclaims to all and sundry the terrible judgement which
is about to befall the nation: their deep-seated sinfulness, for
which they remain quite unashamed, will be met with equally
unrelenting judgement.

9. Imagery derived from the cultivation of vines so familiar
in Palestine is again employed here (cp. 2: 21; 5: 10). As a
grape-gatherer runs his hand over a *vine* to pick any small
clusters of grapes remaining, so the prophet is commanded to
Glean Israel to see if there are any who would receive his
warning. But none can be found. We are reminded here of
5: 1–6, where Jeremiah is commanded to search Jerusalem for
anyone who acts justly but finds none.

10. *Their ears are uncircumcised:* like the *uncircumcised* heart
(cp. 4: 4) the *uncircumcised* ear cannot receive God's word.

13–14. *For all, high and low, are out for ill-gotten gain:* a picture
of widespread social injustice which goes unchallenged by
those whose solemn duty it was to warn and instruct the nation
in the way of God, that is, the *prophets and priests*. In a vivid
image Jeremiah likens them to someone ineffectually treating a
wound, tending it merely superficially with the result that it
will not heal but will deteriorate further and fester. The word
here translated '*All is well*' is the beautiful Hebrew word
shalom, frequently translated 'peace' but much richer in
meaning, designating the harmonious integration of the
powers of nature and of society to produce an ideal condition
for man's life. These *prophets and priests* were thus deluded and
deluding optimists, utter *frauds*. Note that verses 12–15 are
repeated in 8: 10–12. ✻

GOD'S LAW AND HIS PROPHETS SPURNED

16 These are the words of the LORD: Stop at the cross-roads; look for the ancient paths; ask, 'Where is the way that leads to what is good?' Then take that way, and you will find rest for yourselves. But they said, 'We will not.'
17 Then I will appoint watchmen to direct you; listen for
18 their trumpet-call. But they said, 'We will not.' There-fore hear, you nations, and take note, all you who witness
19 it, of the plight of this people. Listen, O earth, I bring ruin on them, the harvest of all their scheming; for they have given no thought to my words and have spurned
20 my instruction. What good is it to me if frankincense is brought from Sheba and fragrant spices from distant lands? I will not accept your whole-offerings, your sacri-
21 fices do not please me. Therefore these are the words of the LORD:

> I will set obstacles before this people
>   which shall bring them to the ground;
> fathers and sons, friends and neighbours
>   shall all perish together.

✲ Although, with the exception of verse 21, these verses are set out as prose in the N.E.B., there is an unmistakable poetic character to this passage as a whole evidenced especially in the use here of the device of parallelism so characteristic of Hebrew poetry. So much is this the case that some other English translations of it (e.g. the Revised Standard Version) set it out as a poetic passage. Whether or not it should be set out as prose, it shows all the signs of being an authentic saying of Jeremiah. In so far as there are some grounds for regarding it as prose, it is possible that an original poetic saying of the prophet has been slightly worked over by a Deuteronomic editor for whom its contents would have been of particular significance (see notes below).

16. *look for the ancient paths:* a reference to God's law given to the nation in ancient times for the right ordering of their life as his people. Deuteronomy was believed to have embodied such law given in ancient times through Moses. Note that in Deuteronomy itself God's law is conceived of frequently as *the way* in which Israel is to walk if the nation is to prosper. It was also a central 'doctrine' in Deuteronomic theology that Israel had rejected God's law; for the Deuteronomic authors the nation had said, as the prophet here puts it, ' *We will not.*'

17. *Then I will appoint watchmen to direct you:* this is a reference to the prophets who were sent by God through the centuries to warn and exhort his people but whose message was spurned. This also was a central feature of Deuteronomic theology (cp., for example, 2 Kings 17: 13). In Ezekiel also the prophet is conceived of as a watchman commissioned to warn the nation of the consequences of its rebellion and sin (cp. Ezek. 3: 17–21; 33: 1–19).

19. *my instruction:* the word here translated is *torah* and was used by the Deuteronomic authors to designate the corpus of laws embodied in the book of Deuteronomy. Thus, whether or not Jeremiah himself had Deuteronomy in mind in using this word or just God's *instruction* in general, a Deuteronomic editor may well have understood it in the specifically Deuteronomic manner as the law.

20. *What good is it to me if frankincense is brought from Sheba?:* this together with what is said in verse 21 is a condemnation of the emptiness and hypocrisy of Israel's cultic worship of God when not matched by a corresponding love for him and obedience to his will in everyday life. Such condemnation is a characteristic feature of the preaching of the prophets in general (cp. e.g. Isa. 1: 10–17; Hos. 6: 6; Amos 5: 21–4; Mic. 6: 6–8). ✳

AGAIN THE PITILESS FOE FROM THE NORTH

22 These are the words of the LORD:

> See, a people is coming from a northern land,
> a great nation rouses itself from earth's farthest
>> corners.

23 They come with bow and sabre, cruel men and pitiless,
> bestriding their horses, they sound like the thunder of
>> the sea,
> they are like men arrayed for battle against you, Zion.

24 We have heard tell of them
>> and our hands hang limp,
> agony grips us, the anguish of a woman in labour.

25 Do not go out into the country,
>> do not walk by the high road;
>> for the foe, sword in hand,
>> is a terror let loose.

26 Daughter of my people, wrap yourself in sackcloth,
> sprinkle ashes over yourself, wail bitterly,
> as one who mourns an only son;
> in an instant shall the marauder be upon us.

* This passage presents yet another vivid description of the advance of the foe from the north. Note that verses 22–3 occur again in 50: 41–2 where they describe an enemy advancing not against Israel but against Babylon. But their usage in ch. 50 is a secondary application of 6: 22–3 where they are to be understood as referring to the Babylonians. We may repeat what we have already observed: in the book as it now stands the foe from the north is identified with the Babylonians and it is very doubtful now whether the sayings concerning this foe ever envisaged any other people.

25. *terror let loose:* the words (*magor-missabib*) are applied as a name to Pashhur by Jeremiah in 20: 3 (cp. the note in the N.E.B. footnote there) where the *terror* in question is explicitly related to the coming Babylonian invasion of Judah. ✶

JEREMIAH AS ASSAYER

I have appointed you an assayer of my people;	27
you will know how to test them and will assay their	
conduct;	
arch-rebels all of them,	28
mischief-makers, corrupt to a man.	
The bellows puff and blow, the furnace glows;	29
in vain does the refiner smelt the ore,	
lead, copper and iron[a] are not separated out.	
Call them spurious silver;	30
for the LORD has spurned them.	

✶ The prophet is likened to a refiner extracting metal from *ore* (29–30). But Jeremiah finds that his attempt to purge the nation of its wickedness is in vain: as a *refiner* casts out impure and useless *ore*, so God has *spurned* his *people*. ✶

False religion and its punishment

✶ Section 7: 1 – 8: 3, which is composed almost entirely in prose, comprises four separate sections as follows: (1) a 'sermon' (7: 1–15) condemning as false the belief that the mere presence of the temple in Jerusalem was a guarantee of the city's inviolability against God's judgement upon Judah's sins. Ch. 26 records that Jeremiah was tried for blasphemy for

[a] copper and iron: *transposed from after* mischief-makers *in verse 28.*

the 'sermon' here reported; (2) a saying inveighing against the practice of the cult of the queen of heaven and other gods (7: 16–20); (3) an oracle condemning the offering of sacrifice as no substitute for obedience to God's commands (7: 21–9); (4) a further saying condemning various pagan practices including human sacrifice (7: 30–1), followed by an oracle of judgement (7: 32–4) which has been supplemented by the addition of 8: 1–3 pronouncing judgement upon the nation's worship of astral gods.

All four passages have it in common that they each, with the partial exception of the third in which verse 29 is poetry, are composed in the style and language of the prose in the book of Jeremiah with recognizably Deuteronomic words and expressions throughout. Snatches of what were probably the original sayings of Jeremiah can be isolated here and there, although it is very doubtful whether any of these original sayings can be reconstructed in anything approaching its entirety, as some commentators have attempted. ✳

THE TEMPLE SERMON

7 THIS WORD CAME FROM THE LORD to Jeremiah.
2 Stand at the gate of the LORD's house and there make your proclamation: Listen to the words of the LORD, all you men of Judah who come in through these gates to
3 worship him. These are the words of the LORD of Hosts the God of Israel: Mend your ways and your doings, that
4 I may let you live[a] in this place. You keep saying, 'This place[b] is the temple of the LORD, the temple of the LORD, the temple of the LORD!' This catchword of yours is a lie;
5 put no trust in it. Mend your ways and your doings, deal
6 fairly with one another, do not oppress the alien, the

[a] *Or, with Vulg.*, I may live with you.
[b] This place: *prob. rdg.; Heb.* Those.

orphan, and the widow, shed no innocent blood in this place, do not run after other gods to your own ruin. Then will I let you live[a] in this place, in the land which I 7 gave long ago to your forefathers for all time. You gain 8 nothing by putting your trust in this lie. You steal, you 9 murder, you commit adultery and perjury, you burn sacrifices to Baal, you run after other gods whom you have not known; then you come and stand before me in 10 this house, which bears my name, and say, 'We are safe'; safe, you think, to indulge in all these abominations. Do 11 you think that this house, this house which bears my name, is a robbers' cave? I myself have seen all this, says the LORD. Go to my shrine at Shiloh, which once I made a 12 dwelling for my Name, and see what I did to it because of the wickedness of my people Israel. And now you have 13 done all these things, says the LORD; though I took pains to speak to you, you did not listen, and though I called, you gave no answer. Therefore what I did to Shiloh I 14 will do to this house which bears my name, the house in which you put your trust, the place I gave to you and your forefathers; I will fling you away out of my sight, as 15 I flung away all your kinsfolk, the whole brood of Ephraim.

✻ Although as it now stands this sermon is a Deuteronomic composition, it cannot be questioned that it is based upon an incident in the prophet's life and on a saying of his on the occasion described. This is clear first of all from the record in ch. 26 of the perilous situation into which his provocative words in this instance brought him. In addition, such striking expressions as the threefold cry of 'the temple of the LORD'

[a] *Or, with Vulg.*, will I live with you.

(verse 4) or the simile likening the temple to 'a robbers' cave' (verse 11) as well as the list of offences (verse 9), so like the decalogue, the Ten Commandments, strike the eye as belonging to the original speech of the prophet upon which the present text has been based. The reason this 'sermon' has been edited by a Deuteronomic editor is that it centres on a theme of great importance in the Deuteronomic theology, the prophetic proclamation of God's law and Israel's rejection of it. Thus already in the book of Deuteronomy Moses is presented as the first of the prophets and the great law-giver who is to be succeeded by a series of prophets whom God would raise up as mediators of his divine will and word to his people Israel (cp. Deut. 18: 15–19; 34: 10). Furthermore, throughout their presentation of the history of Israel after the time of Moses – the corpus of literature Deuteronomy to 2 Kings is now widely regarded as having been composed by Deuteronomic authors who have employed many sources in composing it – these authors have emphasized the role of the prophets as God's spokesmen among his people. Their mission and activity as successors of Moses, proclaiming God's law and exhorting and admonishing Israel to obey it, is summed up in 2 Kings 17: 13: 'the LORD solemnly charged Israel and Judah by every prophet and seer, saying, "Give up your evil ways; keep my commandments and statutes given in the law which I enjoined on your forefathers and delivered to you through my servants the prophets."' Here, in verses 1–15 and in several other similar prose 'sermons' in the book, Jeremiah is portrayed as a prophet in the succession of Moses (cp. the comments on 1: 9). We may note finally that the 'sermon' here follows a pattern: (*a*) proclamation of God's word and law (verses 1–7); (*b*) description of the nation's apostasy and rejection of God's word and law (verses 8–12); (*c*) announcement of judgement (verses 13–15). Other 'sermons' centring on the same theme follow a similar pattern (cp. 11: 1–17; 17: 19–27; 34: 8–22).

2. *Stand at the gate of the LORD's house:* the narrative in

26: 2 records that Jeremiah stood in 'the court of the LORD's house' and we must understand *the gate* referred to here as probably *the gate* separating the outer from the inner court. The people gathered in these courts on fast days and festivals.

4. *This place is the temple of the LORD, the temple of the LORD, the temple of the LORD!:* the belief underlying *this catchword* was that God had chosen Zion and that *the temple* there was his dwelling-place. Such 'doctrines' gave rise to the belief that Jerusalem was inviolable and we can be sure that such an incident as the deliverance of the city from the Assyrians (2 Kings 18: 17 – 19: 37) would have been seen as an emphatic divine endorsement of that belief. It is not difficult to see how such a belief would have developed among the people in general into a fetish. As in other ways, for example with regard to the election of Israel as God's people, the nation all too readily understood the divine election of Zion to be a privilege but failed to understand that it demanded a response on their part of obedience to and love for God. It was for Jeremiah and the few like him to proclaim to the nation that they could not have the one, the privilege, without the other, the responsibility. This is most strongly underlined in Amos 3: 2.

9. We may note the similarity between Israel's offences here stated and some of the Ten Commandments (cp. also Hos. 4: 2).

10. *this house, which bears my name:* according to Deuteronomic theology the temple was not the place where God dwelt; rather his *name* dwelt there, though we must understand the *name* of God to be an extension, so to speak, of the divine personality, just as the *name* of a person in ancient Israel revealed something of its bearer's nature and personality (cp. Deut. 12: 4–5; 1 Kings 8: 27ff.). The presence of this 'name-theology' in this passage is further evidence that it owes its present form to a Deuteronomic editor.

11. *a robbers' cave:* in the incident of the 'cleansing of the temple' in Matt. 21: 13; Mark 11: 17; Luke 19: 46 Jesus is

recorded as having quoted these words of Jeremiah together with words from Isa. 56: 7 (cp. especially Mark).

14. *Therefore what I did to Shiloh I will do to this house:* Shiloh had been one of the major sanctuaries of Israel before the establishment of the monarchy under Saul. The boy Samuel was placed under the custodianship of Eli the chief priest at *Shiloh.* After the defeat of Israel by the Philistines recorded in 1 Sam. 4 and the capture of the Ark which had been housed in the temple at Shiloh, Shiloh ceased to have the importance it hitherto had. Excavations carried out at the ancient site of Shiloh in the 1920s appeared to indicate the destruction of the town about 1050 B.C. and this was taken as evidence of the Philistine defeat of Israel at that time. But more recent excavations and a fresh examination of the archaeological finds of the earlier digs at the site reveal that the town was destroyed much later, possibly by the Babylonians in the time of Jeremiah himself. This being so, it seems probable that the reference here to the destruction of *Shiloh* is to be related to this Babylonian destruction of this ancient town. What Jeremiah was declaring to the people was therefore that just as the sanctity of *Shiloh* as an ancient holy place of God had not saved it from destruction, so also Jerusalem could and would be destroyed unless the nation turned again to God in penitence and obedience. ✶

THE CULT OF THE QUEEN OF HEAVEN

16 Offer up no prayer, Jeremiah, for this people, raise no plea or prayer on their behalf, and do not intercede with
17 me; for I will not listen to you. Do you not see what is going on in the cities of Judah and in the streets of
18 Jerusalem? Children are gathering wood, fathers lighting fires, women kneading dough to make crescent-cakes in honour of the queen of heaven; and drink-offerings are poured out to other gods than me – all to provoke and

hurt me. But is it I, says the LORD, whom they hurt? No; 19
it is themselves, covering their own selves with shame.
Therefore, says the Lord GOD, my anger and my fury shall 20
fall on this place, on man and beast, on trees and crops,
and it shall burn unquenched.

⁂ From the book of Jeremiah (here and 44: 17–19, 25) it
appears that amongst the foreign cults practised in Judah was
that of 'the queen of heaven'. There are difficulties concerning the identity of this goddess and indeed it is not entirely
certain that the Hebrew is to be translated 'the queen of
heaven' though this seems the most probable interpretation of
it. Probably the goddess in question is to be identified with
Astarte (Ashtoreth), the Canaanite goddess of fertility, though
a reference in an Egyptian text to Anat, also a Canaanite
fertility-goddess, might indicate that the cult in question was
of this goddess.

16. *Offer up no prayer, Jeremiah, for this people:* here as in other
places in the book *Jeremiah* is portrayed as one who interceded
for the nation with God (cp. the comments on 14: 7–9, 19–22).

18. *Children are gathering wood, fathers lighting fires, women
kneading dough:* the text pointedly shows the keen involvement
of the people in this cult – men, *women* and even the *Children*
enthusiastically engage in it! *crescent-cakes in honour of the
queen of heaven:* 44: 19 indicates that these *cakes* were stamped
with the goddess's image. Bread was widely used as an offering to gods in ancient Near Eastern religions. In Israel the
'cereal offering' took the form of various kinds of *cakes*,
though it could also consist of an offering of flour alone. ⁂

OBEDIENCE RATHER THAN MERE SACRIFICE

These are the words of the LORD of Hosts the God of 21
Israel: Add whole-offerings to sacrifices and eat the flesh
if you will. But when I brought your forefathers out of 22

Egypt, I gave them no commands about whole-offering
23 and sacrifice; I said not a word about them. What I did
command them was this: If you obey me, I will be your
God and you shall be my people. You must conform to all
24 my commands, if you would prosper. But they did not
listen; they paid no heed, and persisted in disobedience
with evil and stubborn hearts; they looked backwards
25 and not forwards, from the day when your forefathers left
Egypt until now. I took pains to send to them*a* all my
26 servants the prophets; they did not listen to me, they paid
no heed, but were obstinate and proved even more
27 wicked than their forefathers. When you tell them this,
they will not listen to you; if you call them, they will not
28 answer. Then you shall say to them, This is the nation
that did not obey the LORD its God nor accept correction;
truth has perished, it is heard no more on their lips.

29   O Jerusalem, cut off your hair,
        the symbol of your dedication, and throw it
            away;
        raise up a lament on the high bare places.

For the LORD has spurned the generation which has roused
his wrath, and has abandoned them.

* This is yet a further passage in which the mere offering of
sacrifice without loyalty to God's commands is condemned
(cp. 6: 20).
    21. *and eat the flesh if you will:* sacrifice without obedience is
nothing more than the mere eating of *flesh*: it is repugnant to
God when not accompanied with an obedient and willing
heart. Merely to *eat the flesh* brings no communion with God.

[a] *So one MS.; others* you.

22. *But when I brought your forefathers out of Egypt, I gave them no commands about whole-offering and sacrifice; I said not a word about them:* there are two possible ways of understanding this. The first and the one usually accepted by commentators today is that it does not deny the validity of sacrifice or that it was offered from the earliest days of Israel's history but seeks to place the emphasis in Israel's religion on obedience to God's law: it declares 'obedience *rather than* sacrifice' but not 'obedience and no sacrifice', as we may put it. On the other hand, however, the statement is by any standard markedly categorical in nature and one wonders whether it did represent a view in Israel that sacrifices were not essential. Such an understanding of this text might gain some support from the probability that the passage as it now stands was composed during the period of the exile in Babylon or at least with the exiles in Babylon in mind. For these exiles the offering of *sacrifice* was automatically ruled out. Is it possible that this text then represents the attitude of some in exile who came to believe that *sacrifice* was not an absolute essential of their worship of God? Of these two interpretations, the first must be regarded as the more probable, but the possibility of the second should remain open.

25. *I took pains to send to them all my servants the prophets:* on this see the introductory comments on the temple 'sermon' (p. 76). The same statement occurs also in other prose passages markedly Deuteronomic in style and language (e.g. 25: 4).

27. *When you tell them this, they will not listen to you:* Jeremiah will be no more successful than his prophetic predecessors; his message also will be rejected (cp. also, for example, chs. 26 and 36).

29. *cut off your hair:* probably because of its capacity for constant growth, the *hair* was seen as an important seat of life and so of religious significance. One of the conditions for being a Nazirite was to allow the *hair* to grow long (cp. Num. 6: 1ff. Samson let his hair grow long because he was a Nazirite, as we are told in Judg. 13: 5; 16: 17) as a sign of

one's dedication to the Lord. Here Jeremiah demands that Jerusalem *cut off* her *hair* as a sign of her faithlessness to her vows of loyalty to God. ✻

HEINOUS RITES AND OTHER CULTS

30 For the men of Judah have done what is wrong in my eyes, says the LORD. They have defiled with their loath-
31 some idols the house that bears my name, they have built a shrine of Topheth in the Valley of Ben-hinnom, at which to burn their sons and daughters; that was no command
32 of mine, nor did it ever enter my thought. Therefore a time is coming, says the LORD, when it shall no longer be called Topheth or the Valley of Ben-hinnom, but the Valley of Slaughter; for the dead shall be buried in Topheth
33 because there is no room elsewhere. So the bodies of this people shall become food for the birds of the air and the wild beasts, and there will be no one to scare them away.
34 From the cities of Judah and the streets of Jerusalem I will banish all sounds of joy and gladness, the voice of the bridegroom and the bride; for the land shall become desert.
8 At that time, says the LORD, men shall bring out from their graves the bones of the kings of Judah, of the officers, priests, and prophets, and of all who lived in Jerusalem.
2 They shall expose them to the sun, the moon, and all the host of heaven, whom they loved and served and adored, to whom they resorted and bowed in worship. Those bones shall not be gathered up nor buried but shall become
3 dung on the ground. All the survivors of this wicked race, wherever I have banished them,*a* would rather die than live. This is the very word of the LORD of Hosts.

[a] *So one MS.; others add* those who are left.

✶ The practice of human sacrifice referred to here and elsewhere in Jeremiah (cp. note on 2: 23) was the central characteristic of the cult of Molech (cp. Lev. 18: 21; 20: 2–5; 2 Kings
23: 10; and also in other passages, even though the name
Molech is not mentioned), the human sacrifices in question
being children. The Valley of Ben-hinnom appears to have
been its centre, perhaps the only place where it was practised.
The fact that the texts in which it is mentioned are relatively
late suggests that it did not gain a popular footing in Israel
until the late pre-exilic period. In ch. 8, verse 2 refers to astral
cults practised in Judah. There is no need to see these as
having been introduced to Palestine by the Assyrians; there
is plenty of evidence that they were popular cults in Canaan
from well before the coming of the Assyrians in the eighth
century B.C. The same is true of the worship of the sun and
the moon.

31. *Topheth:* literally, 'a burning place', perhaps a reference
to the place where refuse was burnt, but associated, as also in
ch. 19, with alien sacrificial practice.

33. *So the bodies of this people shall become food for the birds of
the air and the wild beasts, and there will be no one to scare them
away:* this expression occurs, with the exception of its final
clause, also in 16: 4 and 19: 7 (cp. also 34: 20) but elsewhere
only in Deut. 28: 26. It must qualify as one of the most gruesome curses in the whole of the Old Testament. ✶

MISCELLANEOUS SAYINGS

✶ The section 8: 4 – 10: 25 comprises a series of separate
sayings composed for the most part in poetry. No single theme
predominates throughout this material, though some individual sayings in it are thematically related. ✶

A SELF-CONFIDENT BUT SELF-DELUDED PEOPLE

4 You shall say to them, These are the words of the
LORD:

> If men fall, can they not also rise?
> If a man breaks away, can he not return?
5 Then why are this people*ª* so wayward,
>   incurable in their waywardness?
> Why have they clung to their treachery
> and refused to return to their obedience?
6 I have listened to them
>   and heard not one word of truth,
> not one sinner crying remorsefully,
>   'Oh, what have I done?'
> Each one breaks away*ᵇ* in headlong career
> as a war-horse plunges in battle.

7 The stork in the sky
>   knows the time to migrate,
> the dove and the swift and the wryneck
>   know the season of return;
> but my people do not know the ordinances of the LORD.
8 How can you say, 'We are wise,
>   we have the law of the LORD',
> when scribes with their lying pens
>   have falsified it?
9 The wise are put to shame, they are dismayed and have
>   lost their wits.
> They have spurned the word of the LORD,
>   and what sort of wisdom is theirs?

[a] *So Sept.; Heb. adds* Jerusalem.   [b] breaks away: *or* is wayward.

84

Therefore will I give their wives to other men   10
    and their lands to new owners.
For all, high and low,
    are out for ill-gotten gain;
prophets and priests are frauds,
    every one of them;
they dress my people's wound,[a] but skin-deep only, 11
    with their saying, 'All is well.'
All well? Nothing is well!
Are they ashamed when they practise their   12
    abominations?
Ashamed? Not they!
They can never be put out of countenance.
Therefore they shall fall with a great crash,[b]
and be brought to the ground on the day of my
    reckoning.
The LORD has said it.
I would gather their harvest, says the LORD,   13
but there are no grapes on the vine,
no figs on the fig-tree;
even their leaves are withered.[c]

✻ The remainder of ch. 8 comprises two main sections both
of which are composed of a number of sayings. The first
consists of two sayings (verses 4–7 and 8–9) deriding the
nation's self-confidence, a further oracle (verses 10–12,
repeated with only minor variations from 6: 12–15) dealing
with the same theme but also announcing judgement, and a

[a] my people's wound: *lit.* the wound of the daughter of my people
(*cp. also 8: 19, 21; 9: 1, 7*).
[b] with a great crash: *or* where they fall *or* among the fallen.
[c] *So Sept.; Heb. adds* so I have allowed men to pass them by.

short saying (verse 13) describing the completeness of the people's apostasy.

4–7. The nation is oblivious of its wrong-doing, clinging to its treachery quite unaware of its rebellion against God. Such behaviour is incredible. Even migratory birds know the simple laws of nature governing their survival. But Israel is ignorant of the laws of God, unnaturally blind to his life-giving commands.

4–6. *If a man breaks away, can he not return?*: the words here translated *breaks away* and *return* as well as the words rendered *wayward, waywardness, to return* (verse 5) and *breaks away* (verse 6) are all derived from the same root in Hebrew, thus making a striking play upon words throughout this passage.

7. We may compare the contrast here drawn between Israel's behaviour and that of animals with the similar contrast described in Isa. 1: 3 where Israel's lack of knowledge of God is contrasted with the ox that knows its owner and the ass that knows its master's stall.

8–9. This short passage is one of the most difficult to understand in the entire book. What is *the law of the LORD* here referred to? Who were the *scribes* here mentioned and of what are they accused? What was the basis of the accusation that they had *spurned the word of the LORD*? It cannot be that the prophet was referring to some bogus law code drawn up by the scribes in question. Nor does it seem credible that he was condemning as false the book of Deuteronomy 'published' in his day, or indeed any other Israelite law code known to us from the Old Testament and in existence at that time (e.g. 'the book of the covenant' in Exod. 20: 22 – 23: 19 or possibly the 'holiness code' in Lev. 17–26). Neither does it seem possible that the reference to *the law of the LORD* being falsified means that these *scribes* deliberately manipulated and distorted it to suit their own ends.

One way of understanding the passage is as follows. The *scribes* were members of the professional class of 'the wise' in

Judah and their particular task in this instance appears to have been concerned with *the law of the LORD.* Since there is a reference here to their *pens* we must assume that they were engaged in writing or composing. This could mean that they prepared written expositions of *the law* for communication to the people, perhaps in the temple during worship. It is not impossible that they were involved to some extent in the composition of Deuteronomy. There is no reason to believe that their intentions were anything but sincere and certainly, if it was Deuteronomy that they were primarily concerned with, the prophet could not have been condemning this book, at least not in itself, as false. It was not, therefore, their activity or intentions or sincerity that Jeremiah was here attacking. What he was condemning was the very theological basis of their teaching and the sort of response it evoked from the nation. It seems that the attitude of these *scribes* to *the law* and their teaching of it was dominated by, and at the same time was aimed at supporting, an orthodoxy which failed to challenge the nation but instead produced complacency. This not only ruled out but positively resisted the ever new, living and demanding word of God which now as at all times entered the nation's life as a disturbing feature. The 'legal piety' which such teaching appears to have led to was seen by Jeremiah to be remote from the inner reality of the situation of the time and to have given rise to a false sense of security among the people with regard to their standing before God and the radical demand his word announced. To this extent the teaching of these scribes stood under the same judgement as that of the false prophets, whom Jeremiah also condemned (cp. chs. 27–8), whose sincerity was also for the most part unquestion-able but whose message to the nation was dictated by an established religious orthodoxy and who were ignorant of the word of God and thus insensitive to the crisis in which the nation stood. As seen by Jeremiah the claim of these *scribes,* and those whom they taught, to be wise was self-delusive, their 'wisdom' was no wisdom at all, their self-confident and complacent piety blinded them to a deeper understanding of God and his purposes for his people, and so, for all their piety and 'religion', their minds and hearts remained closed to the word of God.

10–12. Although these verses are found also in 6: 12–15, they are not inappropriate in this context too, for in so far as they allude to the superficial teaching of *priests* and *prophets* in Jeremiah's day and to the false sense of security they fostered among the nation, they continue the thought of the preceding saying.

13. *even their leaves are withered:* another image of the total apostasy of Israel, here likened to a barren vine or fig-tree, the very *leaves* of which have *withered.* ✽

THE NATION'S RUIN AND THE PROPHET'S SORROW

14 Why do we sit idle? Up, all of you together,
    let us go into our walled cities and there meet our
        doom.
      For the LORD our God has struck us down,
      he has given us a draught of bitter poison;
        for we have sinned against the LORD.
15   Can we hope to prosper when nothing goes well?
      Can we hope for respite when the terror falls
        suddenly?
16   The snorting of his horses is heard from Dan;
    at the neighing of his stallions the whole land trembles.
    The enemy come; they devour the land and all its store,
        city and citizens alike.
17 Beware, I am sending snakes against you,
        vipers, such as no man can charm,
            and they shall bite you.
        This is the very word of the LORD.

How can I bear my sorrow?[a]   18
  I am sick at heart.
Hark, the cry of my people   19
  from a distant land:
'Is the LORD not in Zion?
  Is her King no longer there?'
Why do they provoke me with their images
  and foreign gods?
Harvest is past, summer is over,   20
  and we are not saved.
I am wounded at the sight of my people's wound;   21
I go like a mourner, overcome with horror.
Is there no balm in Gilead,   22
  no physician there?
Why has no new skin grown over their wound?

Would that my head were all water,   **9** 1[b]
  my eyes a fountain of tears,
that I might weep day and night
  for my people's dead!

✴ Section 8: 14 – 9: 1 (in the Hebrew text 8: 23) comprises two originally separate sayings, the first a confession placed on the lips of the people in the face of their imminent destruction, to which has been appended the short saying in verse 17 comparing the coming enemy to deadly snakes, the second a poignant lament by Jeremiah over the destruction of his people (8: 18 – 9: 1).

16. *The snorting of his horses is heard from Dan:* another allusion to the foe from the north (cp. 4: 15).

17. *vipers, such as no man can charm:* an image describing both the deadliness and the inevitability of the coming ruin.

[a] How...sorrow?: *prob. rdg.; Heb. unintelligible.*   [b] *8: 23 in Heb.*

8: 18 – 9: 1. Not for the first time (cp. 4: 19–22) or the last (cp. ch. 14) Jeremiah laments the plight of the nation. Though other prophets suffered the inner agony of the very message they proclaimed, none of their experiences surpassed the grief and turmoil and inner struggle which were the lot of Jeremiah; cp. the note on Jeremiah's 'confessions' on pp. 111–2. The background to the dirge here is the subject of some dispute. Verse 20 has been taken by some as evidence that the poem was occasioned by a drought and resulting famine (cp. also ch. 14). Others believe its background to have been the Babylonian invasion of the country or at least the initial stages of that invasion. Either view is possible. The reference to 'harvest' in verse 20 could be a metaphorical usage and not necessarily an allusion to a drought and famine, whilst the mention of the nation's 'dead' in 9: 1 could refer either to the dead due to famine or to people who had perished at the hands of an enemy. What does seem clear, however, is that the editor who placed this lament in its present context probably understood it as having been uttered by Jeremiah against the background of invasion so clearly presupposed by the poem in verses 14–17.

19. _Is her King no longer there?_: the concept of the kingship of Israel's God Yahweh was one of the dominant religious traditions of ancient Jerusalem and many scholars believe that there was an annual festival held in the temple in the autumn centring on and celebrating the kingship of Yahweh as creator of the world and the sustainer of the nation's life as well as its champion against its enemies. (Psalms such as 93 and 95–9 may have belonged originally to the liturgy of such a festival.)

Why do they provoke me with their images and foreign gods?: this is obviously a secondary addition to the text and is widely recognized as an insertion by a Deuteronomic editor.

22. _Is there no balm in Gilead?_: this _balm_ associated with _Gilead_ is also mentioned in 46: 11 and in Gen. 37: 25. It was an aromatic resin derived from a tree or shrub, but though used widely in ancient times its identity has not been established

with certainty. However, there are no trees in the territory of
what was ancient *Gilead* from which such *balm* could have
been derived and, unless a tree which grew there in ancient
times has subsequently become extinct in this area, it seems
likely that the association of this *balm* with *Gilead* arose because
caravans from the east bearing supplies of it passed through
Gilead. ✢

A DEPRAVED PEOPLE

Oh that I could find in the wilderness a shelter by　　2*a*
　　the wayside,
that I might leave my people and depart!
　　Adulterers are they all, a mob of traitors.
　　The tongue is their weapon, a bow ready bent.　　3
Lying, not truth, is master*b* in the land.
　　They run from one sin to another,
　　　and for me they care nothing.
　　This is the very word of the LORD.

Be on your guard, each man against his friend;　　4
　　put no trust even in a brother.
Brother supplants brother,*c*
and friend slanders friend.
They make game of their friends　　5
　　but never speak the truth;
they have trained their tongues to lies;
deep in their sin, they cannot retrace their steps.
Wrong follows wrong, deceit follows deceit;　　6
　　they refuse to acknowledge me.
　　This is the very word of the LORD.

[a] *9: 1 in Heb.*
[b] not truth, is master: *so Sept.; Heb.* not for truth, they are master.
[c] Brother supplants brother: *or* Every brother is a supplanter like
Jacob (*cp. Gen. 27: 35 and note*).

7   Therefore these are the words of the LORD of Hosts.
     I am their refiner and will assay them.
     How can I disregard my people?
8   Their tongue is a cruel arrow,
     their mouths speak lies.
     One speaks amicably to another,
     while inwardly he plans a trap for him.
9   Shall I not punish them for this?
       says the LORD;
     shall I not take vengeance
       on such a people?

✻ We have already seen how the very mission and message
with which Jeremiah was charged brought him deep sadness
(cp. 8: 18ff.) and we shall come across further poignant outbursts of his inner turmoil later in the book. We shall also see
later how that mission and message incurred for him violent
opposition from his countrymen which on more than one
occasion brought him perilously near to death (cp. e.g. chs. 26,
37, 38). But yet a further thing that brought him intense
sadness and heightened his isolation was his horrified recoil
from the sheer wickedness, deceit and treachery which per-
vaded the society of his time, wickedness, deceit and treachery
which vitiated even the closest relationships. It was this poem of
Jeremiah which William Cowper, appalled by the treachery he
saw all around him in eighteenth-century England, paraphrased
in his poem 'The Time-Piece' (Book Two of *The Task*):

      Oh for a lodge in some vast wilderness,
      Some boundless contiguity of shade,
      Where rumour of oppression and deceit,
      Of unsuccessful or successful war,
      Might never reach me more! My ear is pained,
      My soul is sick, with every day's report
      Of wrong and outrage with which earth is filled.

2. *a shelter by the wayside:* a caravanserai. *shelter* was all such a place afforded. It was otherwise destitute of comfort and amenities, tolerable only for a night's lodging on a journey. To Jeremiah such a place, for all its desolation, was preferable as a place to dwell than Jerusalem, rampant with treachery and a place where one could not trust one's own brother.

3. *The tongue is their weapon:* the emphasis throughout these verses is on the evil and mistrust and treachery so easily committed by the lying *tongue.* Thus *Lying, not truth, is master in the land*; 'friend slanders friend' (verse 4); they 'never speak the truth', and 'they have trained their tongues to lies' (verse 5); 'Their tongue is a cruel arrow, their mouths speak lies. One speaks amicably to another', whilst plotting treachery against him behind his back (verse 8). *for me they care nothing:* the Hebrew is literally 'but me they do not know' (cp. the note on 2: 8). The same verb is used in verse 6 'they refuse to acknowledge me'.

4. *Brother supplants brother:* as the alternative rendering in the N.E.B. footnote indicates, there appears to be an allusion here to Jacob's treachery against his *brother* Esau (the name Jacob is derived from the same root as the word here translated 'supplant', i.e. Jacob = 'supplanter'). Thus the prophet is here claiming that the descendants are like their ancestor, each 'Jacobs' his *brother*!

7–9. For their treachery the people stand under judgement. *I am their refiner and will assay them:* cp. 6: 27–30 (p. 73). ✳

DESOLATION AND RUIN

Over the mountains will I raise weeping and wailing,   10
    and over the desert pastures will I chant a dirge.
They are scorched and untrodden,
        they hear no lowing of cattle;
birds of the air and beasts have fled and are gone.

I will make Jerusalem a heap of ruins, a haunt of wolves,   11
    and the cities of Judah an unpeopled waste.

12 What man is wise enough to understand this, to understand what the LORD has said and to proclaim it? Why has the land become a dead land, scorched like the desert
13 and untrodden? The LORD said, It is because they forsook my law which I set before them; they neither obeyed me
14 nor conformed to it. They followed the promptings of their own stubborn hearts, they followed the Baalim
15 as their forefathers had taught them. Therefore these are the words of the LORD of Hosts the God of Israel: I will feed this people with wormwood and give them bitter
16 poison to drink. I will scatter them among nations whom neither they nor their forefathers have known; I will harry them with the sword until I have made an end of them.

✲ This section comprises a short lament (verse 10) followed by a short oracle of judgement upon Judah and Jerusalem (verse 11) to which has been appended a prose 'commentary' which seeks to explain the destruction of the country. This prose 'commentary' clearly presupposes the devastation of Judah in 587 B.C. It is composed in the characteristic prose style of the book and in both form and content is a Deuteronomic composition. As to its form, it follows the same pattern as 5: 19; 16: 10–13 and 22: 8–9 all of which are also composed in prose and are strikingly similar in style, form and content to Deut. 29: 22–8 and 1 Kings 9: 8–9. This form contains three elements: (*a*) the question asking why destruction has befallen the land; (*b*) the answer and explanation, attributing this destruction to God's judgement upon his people's apostasy; (*c*) a restatement of the circumstances, that is, the devastation of the land, which prompted the question. The text here in verses 12–16 has: (*a*) the question (verse 12); (*b*) the answer and explanation (verses 13–14); (*c*) statement of judgement (verses 15–16). The land had suffered devastation primarily because Israel had forsaken God's law (*torah*) (verse

94

13). This follows the Deuteronomic presentation of Israel's history and downfall as contained in the corpus of literature Deuteronomy to 2 Kings; it was the nation's utter failure to live according to the law given to their ancestors which was its undoing (cp. e.g. 2 Kings 17: 13–23, 34–41; and also the two passages referred to above (Deut. 29: 21–7 and 1 Kings 9: 8–9) which follow the same form and serve the same purpose as this passage in Jeremiah).

10. The note of lamentation is resumed (cp. e.g. 8: 18f.). The picture in this instance is one of the deathly silence of desolation.

12. *scorched like the desert and untrodden:* the prose editor here takes up the phrase in the poetic oracle in verse 10.

15. *I will feed this people with wormwood and give them bitter poison to drink:* wormwood is a plant with a bitter taste and is probably to be identified with a species of the genus *Artemisia*, possibly with its most common species *Artemisia herba-alba Asso*. It is coupled in several other places in the Old Testament, as here, with *bitter poison* (sometimes translated 'gall') which is a poisonous herb the juice of which may have been the 'hemlock' poison drunk by Socrates. They are used here as elsewhere metaphorically for bitterness and tragedy. ✳

WAIL FOR THE DESTRUCTION OF THE LAND!

These are the words of the LORD of Hosts: 17

> [a]Summon the wailing women to come,
>   send for the women skilled in keening
> to come quickly and raise a lament for us,   18
>   that our eyes may run with tears
>   and our eyelids be wet with weeping.
> Hark, hark, lamentation is heard in Zion: 19
>   How fearful is our ruin! How great our shame!
> We have left our lands, our houses have been pulled
>   down.

[a] *So Sept.; Heb. prefixes* Consider and.

20   Listen, you women, to the words of the LORD,
        that your ears may catch what he says.
        Teach your daughters the lament,
        let them teach one another this dirge:
21   Death has climbed in through our windows,
            it has entered our palaces,
        it sweeps off the children in the open air
            and drives young men from the streets.

22 This is the word of the LORD:

      The corpses of men shall fall and lie like dung in the fields,
          like swathes behind the reaper, but no one shall
              gather them.

* Professional mourners are summoned to bewail the
nation's destruction. Death personified as a thief stealthily
enters the houses, both small and great; it sweeps off children
at play outside and youths in the city streets.

17. *Summon the wailing women to come:* mourning rites, including lamentation, were an essential part of the preparation of
the dead for burial and were usually conducted by professional
mourners, chiefly *women*. The description of them as *skilled
in keening*, i.e. 'wailing, lamenting' (the Hebrew is literally
'the wise ones'), probably indicates that professional techniques
and methods as well as what we might call 'trade secrets'
evolved and were employed and handed on by these mourners.

21. This verse is composed in the *qinah* or lament metre
characterized by a first unit (stich) of three beats followed by a
second unit of two beats in each line, the second unit thus
breaking short and creating the effect of a catch in the throat:

    3 Death / has-climbed-in / through-our-windows, /
    2   it-has-entered / our-palaces, /
    3 it-sweeps-off / the-children / in-the-open-air /
    2   and-drives-young-men / from-the-streets. *

MAN'S ONLY GROUNDS FOR BOASTING

These are the words of the LORD: 23

> Let not the wise man boast of his wisdom
> > nor the valiant of his valour;
> let not the rich man boast of his riches;
> but if any man would boast, let him boast of this,   24
> that he understands and knows me.
> For I am the LORD, I show unfailing love,
> > I do justice and right upon the earth;
> > > for on these I have set my heart.
> > This is the very word of the LORD.

⁎ This brief saying stating concisely what men should prize most appears rather abruptly at this point. We can, however, see some connection between it and 9: 2-9. For the man who *knows* (cp. the note on 2: 8) God as one who shows *unfailing love* and does *justice and right upon the earth* is himself a mirror of these divine qualities. As such his relationships with other men and his dealings with them are the very antithesis of those characteristics of the society described in 9: 2-9. Jeremiah's great predecessor Micah summed up in largely the same words as are used here the qualities which God most desires in men (Mic. 6: 8):

> God has told you what is good;
> > and what is it that the LORD asks of you?
> > Only to act justly, to love loyalty,
> > to walk wisely before your God (cp. also Deut. 10: 12).

24. *unfailing love:* cp. the note on 2: 2. ⁎

CIRCUMCISED BUT UNCIRCUMCISED IN HEART

25 The time is coming, says the LORD, when I will punish
26 all the circumcised, Egypt and Judah, Edom and Ammon,
Moab, and all who haunt the fringes of the desert;[a] for all
alike, the nations and Israel, are uncircumcised in heart.

* 26. *Egypt and Judah, Edom and Ammon, Moab:* the Israelites
and these of her neighbours practised circumcision. *all who
haunt the fringes of the desert:* translated in this way (cp. also
25: 23 and 49: 32) this appears to refer to nomadic or semi-
nomadic tribes or clans who lived on the *desert fringes* of the
cultivated land and who also practised circumcision. The
alternative translation noted in the N.E.B. footnote may refer
to desert-dwellers who practised a religious rite involving the
shaving of part of the head, perhaps a rite connected with the
dead. Such rites were banned in Israel (cp. Lev. 19: 27; 21: 5).
uncircumcised in heart: cp. the note on 4: 4. *

GOD AND THE IDOLS OF THE NATIONS

10 Listen, Israel, to this word that the LORD has spoken
against you:

2   Do not fall into the ways of the nations,
        do not be awed by signs in the heavens;
        it is the nations who go in awe of these.
3   For the carved images of the nations are a sham,
        they are nothing but timber cut from the forest,
        worked with his chisel by a craftsman;
4   he adorns it with silver and gold,
    fastening them on with hammer and nails
        so that they do not fall apart.

[a] who...desert: *or* the dwellers in the desert who clip the hair on their
temples.

They can no more speak than a scarecrow in a plot of   5
    cucumbers;
    they must be carried, for they cannot walk.
    Do not be afraid of them: they can do no harm,
      and they have no power to do good.
    Where can one be found like thee, O LORD?   6
Great thou art and great the might of thy name.
Who shall not fear thee, king of the nations?   7
    for fear is thy fitting tribute.
Where among the wisest of the nations and all their
    royalty
    can one be found like thee?
    They are fools and blockheads one and all,   8
    learning their nonsense from a log of wood.
The beaten silver is brought from Tarshish   9
    and the gold from Ophir;[a]
    all are the work of craftsmen and goldsmiths.
    They are draped in violet and purple,
    all the work of skilled men.
But the LORD is God in truth,   10
    a living god, an eternal king.
    The earth quakes under his wrath,
    nations cannot endure his fury.

[You shall say this to them: The gods who did not 11[b]
make heaven and earth shall perish from the earth and
from under these heavens.]

    God made the earth by his power,   12[c]
    fixed the world in place by his wisdom,
    unfurled the skies by his understanding.

[a] *So Pesh.; Heb.* Uphaz.   [b] *Verse 11 is in Aramaic.*
[c] *Verses 12–16: cp. 51: 15–19.*

13   At the thunder of his voice the waters in heaven are
          amazed;[a]
      he brings up the mist from the ends of the earth,
      he opens rifts[b] for the rain
      and brings the wind out of his storehouses.

14   All men are brutish and ignorant;
      every goldsmith is discredited by his idol;
      for the figures he casts are a sham,
      there is no breath in them.

15   They are worth nothing, mere mockeries,
      which perish when their day of reckoning comes.

16   God, Jacob's creator, is not like these;
          for he is the maker of all.
          Israel is the people he claims as his own;
          the LORD of Hosts is his name.

✻ This passage is one of the most scathing and sarcastic
attacks on the worship of idols in the Old Testament. It is
paralleled only by Isa. 44 and in view of the striking similarities
between it and this chapter as well as other passages in Deutero-
Isaiah (Isa. 40–55 come from an anonymous prophet of the
exilic period who is referred to as Deutero-Isaiah) most commentators agree that it was composed in the exilic period and
not by Jeremiah. Like Deutero-Isaiah, for whom a favourite
theme was the great contrast between Yahweh and the lifeless
idols of the nations, the author of this passage sought to show
the Israelites in exile the powerlessness and worthlessness of the
pagan idols by which they were surrounded in Babylon. He
ridicules these idols not only in a biting but also in a highly
humorous manner.

[a] At the thunder…amazed: *prob. rdg.; Heb.* At the sound of his giving
tumult of waters in heaven.
[b] rifts: *prob. rdg.; Heb.* lightnings.

2. *do not be awed by signs in the heavens:* a reference to the Babylonian love of astrology which understood meteors, comets and other celestial phenomena as portents of events to be brought about by the gods on earth.

3. *they are nothing but timber cut from the forest:* cp. Isa. 44: 14–20. The idols are nothing more than the piece of wood from which they are made.

4. *he adorns it with silver and gold:* these verses give a description of how an idol is made. A piece of timber is carved by a craftsman into the required shape of the god, it is overlaid with precious metals such as *silver* or *gold* and then draped with various garments. *so that they do not fall apart:* without the skill of a craftsman with his hammer and nails these 'gods' would *fall apart.* That is the measure of what they really are. The Hebrew could also be rendered 'so that they do not wobble'.

5. *They can no more speak than a scarecrow in a plot of cucumbers:* these 'gods' are as lifeless as a *scarecrow* contrived and put by a peasant in his cucumber patch. So helpless are they that they have to be *carried.* Thus they are dependent upon men not only for their very existence but for movement from one place to another. The implication of all this is that lifeless and helpless pieces of timber such as these idols cannot be gods.

6. *Where can one be found like thee, O LORD?:* though from the beginning exclusive loyalty and worship of Yahweh alone was demanded of Israel this did not mean that the existence of other gods was denied. It was not until the period from which this passage and similar passages in Deutero-Isaiah come that monotheism in the proper sense of the word emerged in Israel. Here Israel's God Yahweh is extolled as the only God, the 'king of the nations' to whom alone worship is due.

7. Nothing to which *the nations* give their worship and devotion can be compared with Yahweh.

8. *learning their nonsense from a log of wood:* a further bitingly sarcastic description of the 'gods' worshipped by the nations.

For all the skill put into their manufacture and adornment, these 'gods' remain mere chunks *of wood*.

9. *Tarshish:* the identity of this place, which is referred to in a number of places in the Old Testament, is not known for certain but many favour the view that it is to be identified with Tartessus in Spain. It may also be a general term. *Ophir:* the location of *Ophir* is not known for certain; it has been located by some commentators in India, by others in Arabia and by still others in Africa. It is chiefly known in the Old Testament as a producer and exporter of gold. Uphaz, which is what the Hebrew text here reads (cp. N.E.B. footnote), is mentioned elsewhere only in Dan. 10: 5 (cp. N.E.B. footnote). The reading adopted by the N.E.B. has the support of the Syriac version of the Old Testament. It is possible, however, that the reading *Ophir* in this version arose as a replacement for Uphaz, a substitution of a well-known source of gold for one whose location was unknown.

10. *a living god:* in contrast to these lifeless pieces of timber, Israel's God is the *living* God, active in the affairs of men, exalted above all and Lord over all. In several ancient Near Eastern religions some gods were thought to suffer death during the course of the annual cycle of nature and subsequently to be revived. Israel shunned any idea that Yahweh was such a dying and rising God.

11. This verse is written in Aramaic, a language which belongs to the same family as Hebrew. It originated as a marginal gloss by a scribe and has subsequently been copied into the body of the text itself. It refers to these idols, created by men and not creators themselves; like the men who made them they also will perish and vanish.

12–16. These verses are also found in 51: 15–19. They may originally have been a separate saying but have been appropriately placed in the present context. Verses 12–13 extol God as creator as against the lifeless idols of the nations. God is the maker of all and Israel is his chosen people.

16. *the LORD of Hosts is his name:* this description of God as

Yahweh Sebaoth may be based upon the belief that Yahweh was *LORD of* the *Hosts* of the stars or of the angels and other heavenly beings. It eventually became an epithet for God's might and power, as here. ✱

IMMINENT EXILE

Put your goods together and carry them out of the   17
   country,
  living as you are under siege.
For these are the words of the LORD: 18
  This time I will uproot
the whole population of the land,
and I will press them hard and squeeze them dry.

  O the pain of my wounds!   19
  Cruel are the blows I suffer.
But this is my plight, I said, and I must endure it.
My home is ruined, my tent-ropes all severed,   20
  my sons have left me and are gone,
  there is no one to pitch my tent again,
   no one to put up its curtains.
  The shepherds of the people are mere brutes;   21
  they never consult the LORD,
  and so they do not prosper,
and all their flocks at pasture are scattered.
Hark, a rumour comes flying,   22
  then a mounting uproar from the land of the north,
an army to make Judah's cities desolate, a haunt of
   wolves.

✱ It is possible that these verses originally followed immediately after 9: 17–22 but were subsequently separated from
it by the insertion of the intervening material. At any rate the

theme of impending doom in 9: 17–22 is continued here. The first part of the passage (verses 17–18) is an oracle announcing imminent exile; verses 19–22 are a lament by the land or Jerusalem, here personified as the 'mother' of its inhabitants, over the impending destruction and exile of the nation. Verse 22 announces the approach of the invading army from the north.

17. *living as you are under siege:* probably the siege which preceded the collapse of Jerusalem to the Babylonians in 597 B.C. is in mind here.

20. Jerusalem, here depicted as a *tent*, bewails her destruction and the exile of her *sons*.

21. *The shepherds:* once again the leaders of the nation (we must, as with other references to *the shepherds*, think in the first place of the kings though the word here may also include others, political as well as religious and cultic leaders) are again pointed to as those ultimately responsible for the plight of the nation as a whole.

22. *a mounting uproar from the land of the north:* a further reference to the 'foe from *the north*' which here, as elsewhere, seems almost certainly to refer to the Babylonians. ✳

A PRAYER FOR MERCY

23   I know, O LORD,
         that man's ways are not of his own choosing;
         nor is it for a man to determine his course in life.

24   Correct us,[a] O LORD, but with justice, not in anger,
         lest thou bring us[a] almost to nothing.

25   Pour out thy fury on nations
         that have not acknowledged thee,
         on tribes that have not invoked thee by name;
       for they have devoured Jacob[b] and made an end of him
         and have left his home a waste.

[a] *So Sept.; Heb.* me.
[b] *So some MSS.; others add* and they will devour him.

✶ 23. *man's ways*, i.e. his destiny, are ultimately under the control of God even though in his pride he may imagine he can do better than God. The underlying belief here is that man's and thus Judah's destiny is entirely under the control of God who can do as he pleases with the nation. There is no resisting God's purposes. The same belief is expressed in 18: 4–6 (cp. also Isa. 45: 9ff.).

24. The prophet prays on behalf of the nation that God would show mercy and patience with his people, correcting their erring behaviour and life and forbearing to destroy them.

25. This verse repeats Ps. 79: 6f. This together with the fact that it is rather loosely connected with what precedes it suggests the probability that a later editor has inserted it into this passage in Jeremiah. It clearly presupposes the destruction of Judah in 587 B.C. and the ensuing exile. ✶

Warnings and punishment

A SERMON ON THE COVENANT

THE WORD WHICH CAME TO JEREMIAH from the **11** LORD: Listen to the terms of this covenant and repeat 2 them to the men of Judah and the inhabitants of Jerusalem. Tell them, These are the words of the LORD the God of 3 Israel: A curse on the man who does not observe the terms of this covenant by which I bound your forefathers 4 when I brought them out of Egypt, from the smelting-furnace. I said, If you obey me and do all that I tell you, you shall become my people and I will become your God. And I will thus make good the oath I swore to your fore- 5 fathers, that I would give them a land flowing with milk and honey, the land you now possess. I answered, 'Amen,

6 LORD.' Then the LORD said: Proclaim all these terms in the cities of Judah and in the streets of Jerusalem. Say, Listen
7 to the terms of this covenant and carry them out. I have protested to your forefathers since I brought them out of Egypt, till this day; I took pains to warn them: Obey me,
8 I said. But they did not obey; they paid no attention to me, but each followed the promptings of his own stubborn and wicked heart. So I brought on them all the penalties laid down in this covenant by which I had bound them, whose terms they did not observe.

9 The LORD said to me, The men of Judah and the inhabitants of Jerusalem have entered into a conspiracy:
10 they have gone back to the sins of their earliest forefathers and refused to listen to me. They have followed other gods and worshipped them; Israel and Judah have broken
11 the covenant which I made with their fathers. Therefore these are the words of the LORD: I now bring on them disaster from which they cannot escape; though they cry
12 to me for help I will not listen. The inhabitants of the cities of Judah and of Jerusalem may go and cry for help to the gods to whom they have burnt sacrifices; they will
13 not save them in the hour of disaster. For you, Judah, have as many gods as you have towns; you have set up as many altars*a* to burn sacrifices to Baal as there are streets in
14 Jerusalem. So offer up no prayer for this people; raise no cry or prayer on their behalf, for I will not listen when they call to me in the hour of disaster.

15   What right has my beloved in my house
          with her shameless ways?

[a] *So Sept.; Heb. adds* altars to the shameful thing.

106

> Can the flesh of fat offerings^{*a*} on the altar
> > ward off the disaster that threatens you?
> Once the LORD called you an olive-tree,   16
> > leafy and fair;^{*b*}
> but now with a great roaring noise
> > you will feel sharp anguish;^{*c*}
> fire sets its leaves alight
> > and consumes^{*d*} its branches.

The LORD of Hosts who planted you has threatened you 17
with disaster, because of the harm Israel and Judah
brought on themselves when they provoked me to anger
by burning sacrifices to Baal.

✻ In our study of the 'temple sermon' in 7: 1–15 we saw
that one of the main themes of the prose in the book of
Jeremiah centres on the prophetic proclamation of the law.
Jeremiah, like the prophets before him throughout Israel's
history (cp. 2 Kings 17: 13), is portrayed in several passages in
the book as one who stood in the succession of Moses the first
prophet and the chief law-giver (cp. Deut. 18: 18f.). Of these
passages 11: 1–17 is undoubtedly the one which most obviously
portrays the prophet in such a role. Here Jeremiah is recorded
as having been commissioned by God to proclaim the
covenant law, 'the terms' of the covenant given to Israel's
ancestors through Moses after the exodus from Egypt. The
fact that it exemplifies so pronouncedly such a favourite theme
of the Deuteronomic literature is itself evidence that this
passage, like 7: 1–15, is, as it now stands, a Deuteronomic
composition. And this is confirmed by the style of the passage,
which indeed is perhaps the most markedly Deuteronomic in

[*a*] fat offerings: *so Old Latin; Heb.* the many.
[*b*] *So Sept.; Heb. adds* the fruit of.
[*c*] you will feel sharp anguish: *transposed from end of verse 15.*
[*d*] consumes: *prob. rdg.; Heb.* they consume.

the entire book (on individual words and phrases see the notes below), as well as by the form it follows (cp. 7: 1–15): after the introduction in verses 1–2 there is (*a*) a proclamation of God's law (verses 3–7); (*b*) a statement of Israel's disobedience (verses 8–10); (*c*) an announcement of God's rejection of, and judgement upon, Israel (verses 11–17).

The purpose of the Deuteronomic authors in composing such a 'sermon' was probably twofold. First, working after the catastrophe which befell Judah and Jerusalem in 587 B.C., they sought to explain why that disaster came about: as in their history of the nation in Deuteronomy to 2 Kings, so here they taught that it was God's judgement upon the nation's utter failure to obey the divine law given to Israel's ancestors after the exodus and constantly proclaimed anew, as in this particular instance by the prophet Jeremiah, to each succeeding generation down through the centuries. But secondly, they sought also to stir their fellow-countrymen, now living in the nation's darkest hour amidst devastation in the homeland itself or in exile in Babylon, to renewed faithfulness to God and to a rededication of themselves to obey his holy law which their fathers had failed to obey. Thus, though it appears to concentrate solely on castigating the nation for its past sins and rebellion against God, this 'sermon' in the context in which it was composed would also have offered hope for the future. For the authors of the prose in the book, like Jeremiah himself, saw beyond the immediate tragedy of the nation to a new future when it would fully realize its calling to be the people of God (cp. the commentary on chs. 24, 29, 30–3, 40: 7 – 44: 30 in vol. 2).

Is this 'sermon' based upon an original saying of Jeremiah as many other prose passages in the book are? Can it be claimed on the basis of this passage that Jeremiah lent his support to the Deuteronomic reform carried out by Josiah in 621 B.C.? The difficulty here is that of the entire passage only verses 15–16, which are composed in poetry, can with any confidence be attributed to Jeremiah. But they have nothing to say, certainly not directly, about the covenant or 'the terms of the covenant'. For the rest the passage is composed throughout in the characteristic Deuteronomic style of the prose in the book. Consequently, if there was an original saying it has been so recast that the actual words of the prophet have disappeared. However, on balance it seems probable that in this instance no such original saying lies behind this passage. It appears, apart from verses 15–16, to be entirely a Deuteronomic composition. As such it represents one important aspect of the Deuteronomic interpretation of the prophetic ministry of Jeremiah, who persistently attacked the sinfulness of the nation, sinfulness which manifested itself in rampant social injustice as well as in the wholesale apostasy to other gods which characterized the cult at that time. In exercising such a ministry Jeremiah was seen by the Deuteronomic authors to have been the spokesman of the covenant, one raised up like many before him as a divinely appointed successor of Moses, the first and greatest of the prophets through whom the covenant law was first mediated to Israel.

2. *the terms of this covenant:* cp. Deut. 29: 1. The *terms* of the *covenant* were the laws laid down to govern Israel's life as God's people in *covenant* with him. In this instance they are the laws contained in the book of Deuteronomy, though it is possible that the Deuteronomic authors of this passage also had in mind earlier collections of laws, most notably the Book of the Covenant in Exod. 20: 22 – 23: 19. A *covenant* was a bilateral agreement or arrangement between two or more parties involving mutual obligations to one another. The parties were not necessarily of equal standing and covenants were often made between a superior and an inferior. Even in such cases, however, the superior also had obligations towards the inferior. A number of texts of treaties between Hittite, Assyrian and other kings and their respective vassals have been discovered. In such treaties (covenants) between a great king and his vassals the vassal was bound under oath to obey the stipulations laid down by the suzerain, whilst the latter as

overlord and as initiator of the treaty was bound, probably also under oath, to certain obligations to the vassal, most notably to protect him against possible enemies. The covenant between God and Israel was also obviously between a superior and an inferior. It was initiated by the superior who laid down stipulations for Israel's observance, at the same time setting forth threats of curse and promises of blessing which would befall Israel according to whether the nation remained faithful to or disobeyed these *covenant* stipulations (cp. Deut. 28). As the listing of blessings itself indicates, God was on his part committed to bestowing his continued blessing upon his (faithful) people, sustaining their life in the land of Canaan and protecting them against their enemies. But notwithstanding the fact that the Old Testament stresses that Israel's relationship with God was solely the result of God's grace and not because of any merit on Israel's part, the *covenant* by its very nature did introduce an element of 'legalism' into Israel's religion. The major question to which this gave rise was how Israel could continue to be God's people if she refused or failed to live according to the *covenant* laws. Could Israel simply be cut off from being the people of God if she failed to obey his will? Or could Israel's sinfulness be overcome so that the curses of the *covenant* would be rendered powerless? The attempt to solve this is contained in the famous 'new covenant' passage in 31: 31-4.

3. *A curse on the man who does not observe the terms of this covenant:* this statement together with the response to it 'Amen' (verse 5) are strikingly similar to Deut. 27: 26: '"A curse upon any man who does not fulfil this law by doing all that it prescribes": the people shall all say, "Amen."'

4. *from the smelting-furnace:* cp. Deut. 4: 20; 1 Kings 8: 51. An obvious metaphor for harsh and bitter affliction.

you shall become my people and I will become your God: sometimes referred to as the 'covenant formula', this expression occurs also in 7: 23; 24: 7 and 32: 38 – all prose passages from the hand of a Deuteronomic author. The Deuteronomic authors were the chief exponents of the covenant between Israel and God and Deuteronomy the clearest and most intense presentation of it in the Old Testament.

5. *the oath I swore to your forefathers:* this may be a reference to the promise made by God to Abraham (cp. Gen. 15) and renewed to Isaac and Jacob, Israel's three great ancestors, or, more probably, simply to those who actually came out of Egypt. *a land flowing with milk and honey:* a familiar description in the Old Testament of the land of Canaan.

7. *I took pains to warn them:* probably a reference to the prophets referred to in similar terms elsewhere in the book (e.g. 7: 25) as having been sent by God through the centuries to warn and admonish his people (cp. 2 Kings 17: 13).

15. *in my house:* that is, in the temple. *Can the flesh of fat offerings on the altar ward off the disaster that threatens you?:* once more the emptiness and uselessness of sacrifice unaccompanied by faithfulness and obedience to God is stressed. The mere offering of sacrifice reduced religion to nothing more than superstition. ✷

JEREMIAH'S 'CONFESSIONS'

✷ Unique in the prophetic books in the Old Testament are a number of passages in the book of Jeremiah (11: 18–23; 12: 1–6; 15: 10–21; 17: 14–18; 18: 18–23; 20: 7–13, 14–18) which give us an intensely personal insight into the prophet's inward turmoil and struggle in the face of the problems and dangers which his life and ministry brought him. These poems, usually designated Jeremiah's 'confessions' though such a description of them is not entirely appropriate, give expression to the struggle in the prophet's mind between faithfulness to his calling and mission on the one hand and the natural feelings and reactions of his heart to the mental and physical distress which his ministry caused him on the other; 'they lay bare the inmost secrets of the prophet's life, his fightings without and his fears within, his mental conflict with adversity and doubt and temptation, and the reaction of his whole nature on a world that threatened to crush him and a task whose difficulty overwhelmed him' (Skinner).

In literary form these 'confessions' display some of the features of a category of Psalms known as 'individual psalms of lament', that is, psalms which appear to have been recited in a cultic setting by individual worshippers in distress and danger who presented their complaint to God and sought deliverance from the plight which had befallen them (e.g. Pss. 3, 5, 6, 7 and many more). Characteristic of these psalms are the worshipper's plaintive description of the peril in which he finds himself, a cry that he has been deserted by God and abandoned to his fate, a protestation of innocence and plea for deliverance, frequently an expression of assurance that God will deliver him, and a prayer that vengeance will be exacted upon his enemies. Often there is a change of mood at the end of such psalms from one of despair to one of confidence and it is probable that between the lament and complaint and this assertion of confidence a cultic official, a priest or cultic prophet, announced an oracle of deliverance and assurance as God's gracious response to the worshipper who has presented his plea before him.

In view of the formal association of Jeremiah's 'confessions' with these psalms, which had their 'setting in life' in Israel's cult, some scholars have argued that Jeremiah was acting not as an individual in composing these laments but was performing a cultic role as an officially appointed spokesman for the people, that is, a cultic prophet. But the intensely personal note which pervades these poems, the knowledge we have from elsewhere in the book concerning Jeremiah's sufferings, as well as the fact that these 'confessions' in places embody responses of God so obviously addressed to Jeremiah as an *individual*, all render such a cultic interpretation of them untenable. That they originated as the outpourings of his own inner struggle cannot seriously be questioned. (On Jeremiah's role as intercessor for the people see also the discussion of his use of the lament form, in this instance the so-called 'communal lament', on 14: 1– 15: 4.) ✻

PLOTS AGAINST JEREMIAH'S LIFE

It was the LORD who showed me, and so I knew; he 18
opened my eyes to what they were doing. I had been like 19
a sheep led obedient to the slaughter; I did not know that
they were hatching plots against me and saying, 'Let us
cut down the tree while the sap is in it; let us destroy him
out of the living, so that his very name shall be forgotten.'

O LORD of Hosts who art a righteous judge,   20
    testing the heart*a* and mind,
    I have committed my cause to thee;
    let me see thy vengeance upon them.

Therefore these are the words of the LORD about the men 21
of Anathoth who seek to take my*b* life, and say, 'Prophesy
no more in the name of the LORD or we will kill you'—
these are his words: I will punish them: their young men 22
shall die by the sword, their sons and daughters shall die by
famine. Not one of them shall survive; for in the year of 23
their reckoning I will bring ruin on the men of Anathoth.

✻ This passage and that immediately following it (12: 1–6)
contain the first two of Jeremiah's recorded 'confessions'. A
problem arises concerning the relationship between this passage
and 12: 1–6, for whilst in 11: 18–23 Jeremiah already knows of
his kinsmen's treachery against him, 12: 6 clearly presupposes
that he is as yet unaware of it. One solution to this problem is
to understand 12: 1–6 as having antedated 11: 18–23. This
proposal has been adopted by several commentators. But

[a] *Lit.* kidneys.   [b] *So Sept.; Heb.* your.

another possibility is that 11: 18–23 is to some extent the work of a Deuteronomic editor. Verses 18–19 must be regarded as Jeremiah's own words. But verses 21–3 show some signs in style and phraseology of having been composed by the authors of the prose in the book. As such they may have been composed as an addition to verses 18–20, interpreting what is said in the light of 12: 6 as a reference to Jeremiah's brothers and kinsmen, the men of Anathoth. If this is so then the original 'confession' may have consisted of verses 18–20, though it is not impossible that the editor was also responsible for placing verse 20 here, borrowing it from 20: 12 where, with minor differences, it also occurs. If verses 18–19 (20) were the original 'confession' they need not necessarily have postdated 12: 1–6.

Taken as it now stands, however, the passage falls naturally into two subdivisions, the prophet's lament and plea (verses 18–20) and God's response to it (verses 21–23).

18–19. Jeremiah laments the treachery plotted against him, describing briefly the intention of his adversaries. So also in the psalms of lament the plaintiff describes, sometimes briefly sometimes at length, the dangers which beset him at the hands of his enemies (e.g. Ps. 3: 1f.). As already noted the crisis in Jeremiah's life to which the 'confessions' witness was his inner struggle between faithfulness to his calling and the natural impulses of his heart. In this particular 'confession' he reveals his poignant reaction to the persecution levelled against him. For any man rejection by, and isolation from, society is one of the heaviest of burdens; for many it is an unbearable cross which quickly breaks their spirit and will. In revealing Jeremiah's deep sense of grief at the rejection and isolation and danger he faced, these 'confessions' show at one and the same time his humanity and his courage. Here was no 'superman' aloof to the mental and physical abuse he suffered, but one whose inner turmoil as much as his physical sufferings drove him at times to seek release from the very divine calling he knew to be his. Yet here also was one who faithfully endured to the end.

20. An expression of confidence in God who vindicates the cause of the innocent is also characteristic of the psalms of lament (cp. e.g. Ps. 17: 1–8), whilst the cry for *vengeance* upon enemies is also typical of them (cp. Ps. 17: 13f.).

21–3. Several other 'confessions' embody God's response to the prophet's lament (cp. 12: 5; 15: 11–12, 19–21 and the note on 20: 13).

21. *the men of Anathoth:* see the note on 1: 1. It has been suggested by several commentators that it was Jeremiah's support for Josiah's reformation that provoked the wrath of his kinsmen at *Anathoth* on the grounds that the centralization of the cult in Jerusalem, involving the suppression of local sanctuaries throughout the land, threatened their livelihood as priests at *Anathoth*. But as we have seen (cp. on 11: 1ff.) it is unlikely that Jeremiah was the active advocate of that reformation which such an understanding of this passage pre-supposes, even though he may have given the reformation his tacit support. Perhaps the reason they sought to *kill* him was because they viewed him, as did many if not most others at that time, as a traitor, one who not only advocated surrender to the nation's deadliest enemy, Babylon, but claimed that the enemy's victory was the very will of God. His kinsmen would have wished at such a time to rid themselves of any suspicion of complicity in, or even sympathy with, his preaching in this respect at least. ✳

WHY DO THE WICKED PROSPER?

O LORD, I will dispute with thee, for thou are just;   **12**
    yes, I will plead my case before thee.
Why do the wicked prosper
    and traitors live at ease?
Thou hast planted them and their roots strike   2
    deep,
    they grow up and bear fruit.

Thou art ever on their lips,
    yet far from their hearts.[a]
3 But thou knowest me, O LORD, thou seest me;
    thou dost test my devotion to thyself.
Drag them away like sheep to the shambles;
    set them apart for the day of slaughter.

4   How long must the country lie parched
        and its green grass wither?
    No birds and beasts are left, because its people are
        so wicked,
    because they say, 'God[b] will not see what we are
        doing.'[c]

5 If you have raced with men and the runners have
        worn you down,
    how then can you hope to vie with horses?
    If you fall headlong in easy country,
    how will you fare in Jordan's dense thickets?
6 All men, your brothers and kinsmen, are traitors to
    you,
    they are in full cry after you;
    trust them not, for all the fine words they give you.

✶ Like the preceding passage, this one also falls naturally into two sections: the prophet's lament and plea (verses 1–3) and God's response (verses 5–6). Verse 4 appears quite out of place here – it looks as though it belonged originally to a context such as 14: 1–6 – and is regarded by most commentators as an insertion, though the last line of it may belong to verse 3.

1. *Why do the wicked prosper?:* Jeremiah may have been the first to experience the burden of this question. But he was not

[a] *Lit.* kidneys.   [b] *So Sept.; Heb.* He.
[c] what we are doing: *so Sept.; Heb.* our latter end.

the only one of his age (cp. Hab. 1: 2–4, 13; Pss. 37, 49, 73;
the problem of the suffering of the just is the central concern
of the book of Job). For the question, which arose from his
reflection on his own suffering as against the success of the
unjust, belongs to the mystery of the reality of evil in God's
creation, a mystery which has confronted men of faith in all
ages.

3. Cp. the comment on 11: 20.

5–6. The only response Jeremiah receives to his lament is
that even worse is to come. Treachery from men in general
is bad enough, but from one's own brethren and family it
acquires an even darker and more tragic dimension and brings
the misery of total isolation and rejection. But if men of faith
have no answer to the problem of evil and suffering, many have
felt themselves drawn closer to God precisely in the midst of
their suffering and have rejoiced in the paradox that God's
purposes triumph in spite of, and even through, the assaults
of evil. Such, in the end, must have been the experience of
Jeremiah. ✶

ISRAEL AND HER NEIGHBOURS

I have forsaken the house of Israel,   7
    I have cast off my own people.
I have given my beloved into the power of her foes.
My own people have turned on me like a lion from   8
    the scrub,
roaring against me; therefore I hate them.
    Is this land of mine a hyena's lair,   9
    with birds of prey hovering all around it?
Come, you wild beasts; come,[a] all of you, flock to
    the feast.

Many shepherds have ravaged my vineyard   10
    and trampled down my field,

        [a] *So some MSS.; others* bring.

they have made my pleasant field a desolate wilderness,

11   made it a waste land, waste and waterless, to my
        sorrow.
The whole land is waste, and no one cares.

12   Plunderers have swarmed across the high bare places in
the wilderness, a sword of the LORD devouring the land
from end to end; no creature can find peace.

13   Men sow wheat and reap thistles;
        they sift but get no grain.
        They are disappointed of their*a* harvest
        because of the anger of the LORD.

14   These are the words of the LORD about all those evil
neighbours who are laying hands on the land which I
gave to my people Israel as their patrimony: I will uproot
16*c* them from that*b* soil. Yet, if they will learn the ways of
my people, swearing by my name, 'By the life of the
LORD', as they taught my people to swear by the Baal,
17 they shall form families among my people. But if they
will not listen, I will uproot that people, uproot and destroy them. Also I will uproot Judah from among them;
15 but after I have uprooted them, I will have pity on them
again and will bring each man back to his patrimony and
his land. This is the very word of the LORD.

✻ The remainder of ch. 12 comprises a poem expressing
God's lamentation over the devastation wrought upon his
people and their land by invading enemies (verses 7–13) to
which has been appended a saying in prose from an editor

[*a*] *Prob. rdg.; Heb.* your.   [*b*] *Prob. rdg.; Heb.* their.
[*c*] *The rest of verse 14 and verse 15 transposed to follow* destroy them *in
verse 17.*

concerning Israel's neighbours who had attacked her (verses 14–17). The background of the former is probably the invasion of Judah in 602 B.C. by marauding bands of Babylonians, Aramaeans, Moabites and Ammonites sent against Jehoiakim because of his rebellion against Nebuchadrezzar (2 Kings 24: 2). The devastation wrought by these enemies is seen as God's judgement upon his people's rejection of him. The mood changes abruptly in verses 14–17. Here these 'evil neighbours' of the nation, although in verses 7–13 the instrument of God's judgement upon his people, are seen as God's enemies as well. Yet they too may receive God's mercy if they turn to him and abandon the gods which they have hitherto worshipped. The 'universalist' thinking of this passage, that is, the idea that foreign nations could become worshippers of Yahweh (cp. 3: 17; 18: 7–10, which are also prose passages from an editor), as well as the probability (cp. verses 14*b*–15) that the exile is presupposed, support the view that this prose passage derives from an editor, probably the Deuteronomic author whose hand is so much in evidence throughout the prose passages in the book. The Jewish historian Josephus (first century A.D.) records that the Babylonians subjugated the Ammonites and Moabites in 582 B.C. and it is possible that Edom was destroyed at the same time. If this information is reliable, it is possible that this passage presupposes these events.

7. *the house of Israel:* the Hebrew is 'my house' but the context makes it clear that this refers to the nation and not in this instance to the temple. *my own people:* the Hebrew is literally 'my heritage', a familiar designation of *Israel* as the *people* of God in the Old Testament.

9. *a hyena's lair:* the image is one of vultures hovering, waiting to swoop down and devour what they can of what is left of a carcass of an animal killed by the *hyena*.

10. *Many shepherds:* that is, kings of foreign nations. *my vineyard:* cp. 2: 21 and 5: 10.

14. *I will uproot them:* on the use of this and related terminology see the comment on 1: 10.

16. *the ways of my people:* that is, the worship of Israel's God Yahweh, as the ensuing expression *swearing by my name, 'By the life of the LORD'* indicates. To invoke or swear by the name of Yahweh implied and presupposed that the person making the oath worshipped him. *they shall form families:* literally 'they shall be built up'. The verb here used is the same as that translated 'to build' in 1: 10 (see the comment there).

14*b*–15. The transposition of these verses to follow 17 makes better sense of the passage. As already noted, what is here stated, especially *I will have pity on them again and will bring each man back to his patrimony and his land*, appears to presuppose the exile of 587 B.C. ✳

A SYMBOLIC ACT WITH A LINEN GIRDLE

13 These were the words of the LORD to me: Go and buy yourself a linen girdle and put it round your waist, but do 2 not let it come near water. So I bought it as the LORD had 3 told me and put it round my waist. The LORD spoke to me 4 a second time: Take the girdle which you bought and put round your waist; go at once to Perath and hide it in a 5 crevice among the rocks. So I went and hid the girdle at*a* 6 Perath, as the LORD had told me. After a long time the LORD said to me: Go at once to Perath and fetch back 7 the girdle which I told you to hide there. So I went to Perath and looked for the place where I had hidden it, but when I picked it up, I saw that it was spoilt, and no good 8, 9 for anything. Again the LORD spoke to me and these were his words: Thus will I spoil the gross pride of Judah, the 10 gross pride of Jerusalem. This wicked nation has refused to listen to my words;*b* they have followed other gods,

[a] *Or* by.
[b] *So Sept.; Heb. adds* which has followed the promptings of its stubborn heart.

serving them and bowing down to them. So it shall be[a]
like this girdle, no good for anything. For, just as a girdle 11
is bound close to a man's waist, so I bound all Israel and all
Judah to myself, says the LORD, so that they should become
my people to win a name for me, and praise and glory;
but they did not listen.

* This passage records a symbolic act or, as it has also been
described, an acted parable in which Jeremiah portrayed and
announced God's rejection of his people. Like other symbolic
acts recorded in the book (see the commentary on ch. 19 : 10 and
cp. also chs. 27 and 28) the act was not merely an illustration or
'visual aid', so to speak, but was believed to be imbued, like
the prophetic word itself, with power to effect what it
symbolized. So here Jeremiah uses a linen girdle to enact the
inevitable judgement of God upon the nation: just as the linen
girdle was spoiled so also would 'the gross pride of Judah, the
gross pride of Jerusalem' (verse 9) be spoiled. The description
of the parable in its original form is contained in verses 1–9,
verses 10–11 being a secondary expansion of it by a Deuteronomic author.

1–5. For the first part of this symbolic act Jeremiah, at the
command of God, purchases *a linen girdle* and, having worn it
for some time, takes it, again at the command of God, and
hides it at *Perath*. The word here rendered *Perath* is also the
word for the Euphrates elsewhere in the Old Testament, and
other English versions as well as many commentators translate
it as Euphrates in the present context. Against this it has been
argued that to have gone to the Euphrates would have involved
two round trips of some 700 miles (about 1,126 km) each for
Jeremiah and that, in addition, part of the point of the symbolic act would have been missed since no one in Judah would
have gone with him to witness his concealment of the *girdle*
or his later retrieval of it. Hence it is argued that the place in

[a] *Prob. rdg.; Heb.* And let it be.

question was *Perath*, which is but a few miles northeast of Anathoth. At the same time the very choice of *Perath* was simply because its name was identical with that of the Euphrates so that it was seen to symbolize, for the purpose of the prophet's parable here, the Euphrates.

6–9. For the second part of this symbolic act Jeremiah, once more at the command of God, returns to *Perath* and retrieves the hidden *girdle* only to find that it has in the meantime been *spoilt*, that is, has rotted and is now useless. This is followed by the interpretation of the symbolic act: as this linen *girdle* has been spoiled so also will *the gross pride of Judah, the gross pride of Jerusalem* be destroyed.

Understood in this way, the symbolic act here described appears to concern the nation's exile, here announced by Jeremiah in the darkest possible colours. As the linen *girdle* purchased and worn by Jeremiah was subsequently carried away to *Perath* there to rot and decay into uselessness, so also *Judah* would be carried into exile, put away by God, beyond the Euphrates (Perath!) to its doom. Against such an interpretation of this passage it may be objected that such a portrayal of unmitigated doom upon the nation is sharply at variance with one of the main themes of Jeremiah's preaching, namely, the message that after judgement (exile) God would bring about a renewal of the nation. But the same could be said of not a few other passages in the book which likewise announce unmitigated judgement upon the nation and, besides, it cannot be expected that Jeremiah or any other prophet should include his entire message in each individual saying. We must clearly make allowance for the intensity of the prophet's message of judgement to have varied from one situation to another.

10–11. These verses are an editorial expansion and interpretation of the preceding symbolic act. Their phraseology links them unmistakably with other passages in the book which derive from Deuteronomic authors (cp. especially verse 11 with Deut. 26: 19). Note that the expression 'which has followed the promptings of its stubborn heart' (N.E.B.

footnote) occurs frequently in the prose sections of the book. We may query its relegation to a footnote in the N.E.B. The fact that it is not found in the Septuagint is not a sufficient basis for omitting it, for there are numerous places in the book as a whole where the Septuagint has a shorter, in some places a considerably shorter, text than the Hebrew, which must be regarded as a more fully developed presentation of Jeremiah's message (see p. 15f.). *

THE PARABLE OF THE JARS

You shall say this to them: These are the words of the 12 LORD the God of Israel: Wine-jars should be filled with wine. They will answer, 'We know quite well that wine-jars should be filled with wine.' Then you shall say to 13 them, These are the words of the LORD: I will fill all the inhabitants of this land with wine until they are drunk— kings of David's line who sit on his throne, priests, prophets, and all who live in Jerusalem. I will dash them to 14 pieces one against another, fathers and sons alike, says the LORD, I will show them no compassion or pity or tenderness; nor refrain from destroying them.[a]

* Though it appears to be addressed to the same audience as in the previous passage, the content of this parable of the jars marks it off as an originally independent saying of Jeremiah. He may here have taken up a popular proverb, *wine-jars should be filled with wine*, to the effect that everything has its function and intended use. But Israel is fit for nothing but destruction. So, using further the imagery of the proverb, Jeremiah announces that God would fill the people with the *wine* of his wrath and then destroy them, just as *wine-jars* may be dashed *to pieces* by being smashed *one against another*. *

[a] nor refrain...them: *or* so corrupt are they.

A PLEA AND A WARNING

15 Hear and attend. Be not too proud to listen,
      for it is the LORD who speaks.
16 Ascribe glory to the LORD your God
      before the darkness falls,
    before your feet stumble
      on the twilit hill-sides,
    before he turns the light you look for
      to deep gloom and thick darkness.
17 If in those depths of gloom you will not listen,
    then for very anguish I can only weep and shed tears,[a]
    my eyes must stream with tears;
      for the LORD's flock is carried away into captivity.

✣ The image is one of shepherds who have guarded their
flocks (cp. verse 17) on the hill-sides during the night and now
await the dawn and the coming of day. But for God's people,
his flock, the twilight of gloom in which they now find themselves will not turn to the light of day unless, even at this late
hour, they repent and turn again to God. That twilight, far
from being followed by the light of day, will be seen to have
been but 'the waning light of the day of grace' (Skinner).
The background to this saying may have been the deportation
of 597 B.C. even after which there was still time for a change
of heart in the nation. What happened then was but the twilight compared with the darkness of the catastrophe which
was to follow in 587 B.C.

    15. *Be not too proud to listen:* a plea to a self-willed and
conceited nation which had through the years poured scorn
on God's message brought by the prophets.

[a] If...shed tears: *or* If you will not listen to this, for very anguish I
must weep in secret.

17. *then for very anguish I can only weep and shed tears:* this verse contains a further expression of Jeremiah's deep sorrow over the fate of his people (cp. 4: 19f.; 8: 18f.; 9: 1). ✳

A DIRGE OVER THE KING AND THE QUEEN MOTHER

Say to the king and the queen mother:*a*   18
  Down, take a humble seat,
for your proud crowns are fallen from your heads.*b*
  Your cities in the Negeb are besieged,   19
  and no one can relieve them;
  all Judah has been swept into exile,
    swept clean away.

✳ This short poem is a dirge, written in the *qinah* metre (cp. the comment on 9: 21), which was almost certainly composed concerning the fate of Jehoiachin and his mother (cp. also 22: 26; 29: 2). Jehoiachin became king at the age of eighteen in succession to Jehoiakim who died during the Babylonian siege of Jerusalem in 598 B.C. The young king reigned for only three months and was taken into exile to Babylon after the collapse of Jerusalem to Nebuchadrezzar in 597 B.C. (2 Kings 24: 8ff.). He was released from prison in exile in 562 B.C. but was never permitted to return home (cp. 2 Kings 25: 27–30 = Jer. 52: 31–4).

18. The *queen mother*'s name was Nehushta (2 Kings 24: 8). The fact that she is mentioned here is not merely because she would have had influence over her young son, but because the *queen mother* in Judah probably had an official status. The *queen mother* may have worn a crown, as this verse appears to indicate, whilst 1 Kings 2: 19 suggests that she had a throne adjacent to that of the king. The mention of the names of the

[a] *Or* queen.
[b] from your heads: *so Sept.; Heb.* your pillows.

mothers of most of the Judaean kings in the books of Kings might also indicate the importance of *the queen mother* in the Judaean royal establishment.

19. *the Negeb:* properly the largely waterless territory south of *Judah.* Here it seems to be used as simply a reference to the south of *Judah* itself. ✲

THE PORTION OF THE REBEL

20   Lift up your eyes and see
         those who are coming from the north.
     Where is the flock that was entrusted to you,
         the flock you were so proud of?
21   What will you say when you suffer
         because your leaders*a* cannot be found,
     though it was you who trained them
         to be your head?
     Will not pangs seize you,
         like the pangs of a woman in labour,
22   when you wonder,
     'Why has this come upon me?'
     For your many sins your skirts are torn off you,
         your limbs*b* uncovered.

23   Can the Nubian change his skin,
         or the leopard its spots?
     And you? Can you do good,
         you who are schooled in evil?
24   Therefore I will scatter you*c* like chaff
         driven by the desert wind.

[a] leaders: *transposed from next line.*
[b] *Lit.* heels.
[c] *Prob. rdg.; Heb.* them.

This is your lot, the portion of the rebel,[a]   25
   measured out by me, says the LORD,
   because you have forsaken me
   and trusted in false gods.
So I myself have stripped off your skirts   26
   and laid bare your shame.
Your adulteries, your lustful neighing,   27
your wanton lewdness, are an offence to me.[b]
   On the hills and in the open country
   I have seen your foul deeds.
Alas, Jerusalem, unclean that you are!
How long, how long will you delay?[c]

* This poem concerning the approaching judgement of
Jerusalem may have been composed in 605 B.C. when the
Babylonians defeated the Egyptians at Carchemish and were
soon to subjugate Judah. For Judah the events of that year were
the beginning of the end. In the years of turmoil and tragedy
which lay ahead the nation would reap the reward of its
rebellion against God.

20. *those who are coming from the north:* the foe from *the north*
already vividly described in previous poems. *the flock:* Jerusalem is personified as a shepherdess, guardian of God's *flock.*

21. *because your leaders cannot be found:* Jeremiah was
relentless in his indictment of the nation's *leaders*, both the
kings and the political officials of the day as well as the cultic
'establishment'.

22. *For your many sins your skirts are torn off you:* what is about
to befall the nation is the richly deserved punishment for all
its *sins*. There may be an allusion to the stripping of an
adulterous woman, as also in Hos. 2: 3.

    [a] rebel: *prob. rdg., cp. Sept.; Heb.* measures.
    [b] an offence to me (*Heb.* you): *transposed from verse 26.*
    [c] How...delay?: *prob. rdg.; Heb. unintelligible.*

23. *Can the Nubian change his skin, or the leopard its spots?:* so deep-seated and ingrained is Judah's sinfulness that it has virtually become an unalterably fixed feature of its life and behaviour.

27. Once again the imagery of adultery is employed to describe the nation's worship of Baal, a dominant aspect of which involved sexual practices in connection with fertility rites. *On the hills:* that is, the 'high-places', the Baal sanctuaries throughout the land. ✳

JUDAH'S HOPELESS PLIGHT

✳ The passage 14: 1 – 15: 4 comprises two separate sections which are, however, very similar in both nature and form. The first consists of a lament in poetic form (14: 1–9) followed by a prose passage (verses 10–16), and the second likewise begins with a lament in poetic form (verses 17–22) which is followed by a further prose passage in this case incorporating a short poetic saying as well (15: 1–4). The laments are in each case from Jeremiah himself, whilst the prose passages, though incorporating his words, owe their present form to a Deuteronomic author.

Though spoken by Jeremiah himself, it will be noticed that the first person plural form of address is employed in the laments in addition to the first person singular (14: 7–9, 19–22). In this way the prophet identifies himself with the nation, becoming its 'mouthpiece', presenting its plight to God and interceding on its behalf for deliverance from the tragedies which have befallen it. We have already come across allusions to Jeremiah's intercessory role (7: 16; 11: 14; cp. 4: 10) and these two poetic passages provide concrete examples of that role. This together with the fact that the two poems in question in both form and substance belong to the liturgical category of the lament, specifically the so-called 'communal lament', of which there are many examples in the Psalms, might suggest that Jeremiah exercised an official cultic role in the temple, that is, that he was at least at some stage in his ministry a cultic prophet. But the evidence we have from elsewhere in the book is strongly against this, for Jeremiah probably more than any of the other great prophets was rejected and isolated by his contemporaries in Jerusalem and not least of all by the cultic authorities in the temple (cp. for example 20: 1–6; 26: 7–19; 36: 5). Accordingly, it seems more likely that, although he did intercede for the people and in doing so employed conventional liturgical forms, he did so as one deeply and passionately caught up by his own individual calling in the fate and suffering of the nation and not as the holder of an office in the Jerusalem cultic establishment (cp. also the comments concerning Jeremiah's 'confessions' on pp. 111f. above). ✷

LAMENT AND SUPPLICATION IN TIME OF DROUGHT

This came to Jeremiah as the word of the Lord **14** concerning the drought:

Judah droops, her cities languish,   2
> her men sink to the ground;
> Jerusalem's cry goes up.
Their flock-masters send their boys for water;   3
they come to the pools but find no water there.
> Back they go, with empty vessels;[a]
> the produce[b] of the land has failed,   4
> because there is no rain.[c]
> The farmers' hopes are wrecked,
> they uncover their heads for grief.

[a] *So Sept.; Heb. adds* disappointed, shamed, and with uncovered heads.
[b] the produce: *prob. rdg.; Heb. obscure.*
[c] *So Sept.; Heb. adds* in the land.

5   The hind calves in the open country
        and forsakes her young
      because there is no grass;
6   for lack of herbage, wild asses stand on the high bare
          places
      and snuff the wind for moisture,
      as wolves do, and their eyes begin to fail.
7   Though our sins testify against us,
      yet act,[a] O LORD, for thy own name's sake.
    Our disloyalties indeed are many; we have sinned
        against thee.
8   O hope of Israel, their saviour in time of trouble,
    must thou be a stranger in the land,
      a traveller pitching his tent for a night?
9   Must thou be like a man suddenly overcome,
      like a man powerless to save himself?
      Thou art in our midst, O LORD,
    and thou hast named us thine; do not forsake us.

10   The LORD speaks thus of this people: They love to stray from my ways, they wander where they will. Therefore he has no more pleasure in them; he remembers their 11 guilt now, and punishes their sins. Then the LORD said to 12 me, Do not pray for the well-being of this people. When they fast, I will not listen to their cry; when they sacrifice whole-offering and grain-offering, I will not accept them. I will make an end of them with sword, with famine and 13 pestilence. But I said, O Lord GOD, the prophets tell them that they shall see no sword and suffer no famine; for thou wilt give them lasting prosperity in this place.

               [a] *Or* turn away.

The LORD answered me, The prophets are prophesying 14
lies in my name. I have not sent them; I have given them
no charge; I have not spoken to them. The prophets offer
them*a* false visions, worthless augury, and their own
deluding fancies. Therefore these are the words of the 15
LORD about the prophets who, though not sent by me,
prophesy in my name and say that neither sword nor
famine shall touch this land: By sword and by famine shall
those prophets meet their end. The people to whom they 16
prophesy shall be flung out into the streets of Jerusalem,
victims of famine and sword; they, their wives, their sons,
and their daughters, with no one to bury them: I will
pour down upon them the evil they deserve.

✲ As already noted, verses 1–9 in both form and substance
belong to the liturgical category of the lament (see the
analysis below). God's response to this lament and supplication
is contained in verse 10. Verses 11–16 continue this response,
further announcing judgement, then moving to a condemnation of false prophets.

1–6. Characteristic of a lament in time of national distress or
disaster was a description of the plight of the nation. Often such
plight was due to invasion and defeat by an enemy (cp. e.g.
Ps. 74: 4–8). Here Jeremiah describes in some detail a disaster
which has befallen the nation as the result of a terrible drought.

7. In pleading for help and deliverance the prophet, at this
point identifying himself with the nation, confesses to God the
nation's past rebellion against God (cp. e.g. Ps. 79: 8f.;
Lam. 1: 18, 20).

8–9 a. Also characteristic of laments was the plaintive
question addressed to God: has God forsaken his people
completely? Why has he brought such disaster upon his

[a] *So some MSS.; others* you.

people? Surely God who has wrought deliverance for the nation in times past will now act again? (cp. e.g. Ps. 44: 23f.).

9 *b*. For obvious reasons supplication is also a characteristic of laments: the nation cries out to God for deliverance from the disaster which has overtaken it (cp. e.g. Ps. 44: 26).

10. There is evidence that after the singing of a lament a cultic official, whether a priest or a cultic prophet, pronounced an oracle of deliverance to the congregation or, in the case of an individual lament, to the petitioner in question. In the nature of the case not many such oracles of assurance have been preserved, since they were not a part of the lament proper. But that such oracles were delivered would account for the sudden change from despair to confidence which sometimes occurs at the end of a psalm of lament; we may assume that between the lamentation and petition such oracles were given, after which the worshipper expressed his confidence in his deliverance by God (e.g. Ps. 6: 8–10). A few psalms embody such oracles of assurance and deliverance (cp. Pss. 12: 5; 60: 6–8; 91: 14–16). The formal relationship of this verse to the lament which precedes it may be understood on the basis of this. But here instead of the oracle of assurance which normally followed laments there is a statement of judgement which thus becomes all the more effective.

11–16. This section is a Deuteronomic addition to, and development of, Jeremiah's words which precede it. The judgement announced in verse 10 and presupposed in the lament itself is here further stressed. But the main content of it is an attack on false prophecy. We have already come across condemnations of false *prophets* by Jeremiah himself (2: 8; 4: 9; 5: 13; 6: 13). False prophecy appears to have been a major problem of the time (cp. Deut. 18: 20–2) and remained so during the period of the exile as the intense concern with it in a number of prose passages in the book testify (cp. 23: 16–40; 27; 28; 29: 15–23). ✶

LAMENT AND SUPPLICATION IN TIME OF
DEFEAT AND FAMINE

So this is what you shall say to them: 17
Let my eyes stream with tears,
ceaselessly, day and night.
For the virgin daughter of my people
has been broken in pieces,
struck by a cruel blow.
If I go out into the country,   18
I see men slain by the sword;
if I enter the city, I see the ravages[a] of famine;
prophet and priest alike
go begging round the land and are never at rest.
Hast thou spurned Judah utterly?   19
Dost thou loathe Zion?
Why hast thou wounded us, and there is no remedy;
why let us hope for better days, and we find nothing
good,
for a time of healing, and all is disaster?
We acknowledge our wickedness,   20
the guilt of our forefathers;
O LORD, we have sinned against thee.
Do not despise the place where thy name dwells   21
nor bring contempt on the throne of thy glory.
Remember thy covenant with us and do not make it
void.
Can any of the false gods of the nations give   22
rain?
Or do the heavens send showers of themselves?

[a] *Lit.* ulcers.

133

> Art thou not God, O LORD,
> that we may hope in thee?
> It is thou only who doest[a] all these things.

15 The LORD said to me, Even if Moses and Samuel stood before me, I would not be moved to pity this people.
2 Banish them from my presence; let them be gone. When they ask where they are to go, you shall say to them, These are the words of the LORD:

> Those who are for death shall go to their death,
> and those for the sword to the sword;
> those who are for famine to famine,
> and those for captivity to captivity.

3 Four kinds of doom do I ordain for them, says the LORD: the sword to kill, dogs to tear, birds of prey from the skies and beasts from their lairs to devour and destroy.
4 I will make them repugnant to all the kingdoms of the earth, because of the crimes of Manasseh son of Hezekiah, king of Judah, in Jerusalem.

☆ This section is obviously closely similar in nature and form to the preceding. It comprises a lament, and in this instance the background appears to be defeat and famine, followed by a prose passage incorporating a poetic saying and recording God's response to the prophet's lament and supplication. Probably the poetic saying in 15: 2 is the original saying of Jeremiah, but the remainder of 15: 1–4 is from a Deuteronomic author (see notes below).

17–18. As in the case of the lament in 14: 1–6, this one also begins with a poignant description of the plight of the nation. Defeat at the hands of an enemy is associated with famine

[a] *Or* madest.

which so frequently came in the wake of the ravages of war.
The historical background is possibly the Babylonian invasion
of Judah in 597 B.C. with its resultant devastation and exile
(cp. 15: 2).

19. Again, as in the case of 14: 8–9 *a*, the plaintive question
addressed to God occurs.

20. The prophet, identifying himself with the nation, confesses its sin against God (cp. 14: 7).

21–2. The characteristic petition or supplication follows,
accompanied as so often in psalms of lament by a hymnic
allusion to the mercy and greatness of God (e.g. Ps. 74:
12–17).

15: 1–4. The poetic saying in verse 2 is probably the original
response to the lament in 14: 17–22 and, as in the case of the
response in 14: 10, it is an oracle of judgement instead of the
oracle of assurance and deliverance which normally followed
laments in their liturgical setting. Verse 1 is from a Deuteronomic author. Even the prayers of Jeremiah's illustrious predecessors (see the comment on 1: 9 and cp. Deut. 9: 13–29;
1 Sam. 12: 19–25) would be of no avail in the present circumstances, so deep is the nation's sin and so irrevocable the judgement of God upon it. Verses 3–4 are likewise a Deuteronomic
composition. In the Deuteronomic history *Manasseh* is singled
out as one who as much as any and more than most fostered
and led the nation's apostasy (cp. 2 Kings 21: 11–17; 23: 26;
24: 3). For the phraseology employed in these two verses see
Deut. 28: 25–6. ✳

WHO WILL TAKE PITY ON YOU, JERUSALEM?

> Who will take pity on you, Jerusalem,   5
>   who will offer you consolation?
> Who will turn aside to wish you well?
> You cast me off, says the LORD,   6
>   you turned your backs on me.

So I stretched out my hand and ruined you;
  I was weary of relenting.
7   I winnowed them and scattered them
    through the cities of the land;
  I brought bereavement on them, I destroyed my
      people,
    for they would not abandon their ways.
8   I made widows among them more in number
    than the sands of the sea;
  I brought upon them a horde of raiders[a]
    to plunder at high noon.
  I made the terror of invasion fall upon them
    all in a moment.
9   The mother of seven sons grew faint,
    she sank into a swoon;
  her light was quenched while it was yet day;
    she was left humbled and shamed.
  All the remnant I gave to perish by the sword
    at the hand of their enemies.
  This is the very word of the LORD.

✶ In view of its beginning as well as its content this poem,
though originally separate, has been aptly placed after the
preceding material, the main theme of which it continues:
God's punishment of his rebellious people is unrelenting.
Though the perfect tense, which is employed here, is very
often used for predicting the future (it is usually referred to as
the 'prophetic perfect'), it seems probable that in this instance
the poem is dealing with a tragedy which has already befallen
the nation. Since the imagery employed describes the ravages
and tragedies of invasion and war, the background to the
poem is probably the Babylonian invasion of Judah in 597 B.C.

[a] I brought...raiders: *prob. rdg.; Heb. obscure.*

It is less likely that it presupposes the invasion of 601 B.C., though this is not impossible, while if the catastrophe of 587 B.C. was in mind we would have expected an even more intensified description of the dire results and in particular probably a more detailed or heightened description of the fate of Jerusalem itself at that time.

5. The note of lamentation here serves to link this poem with the material which precedes it.

7. *I winnowed them and scattered them:* it is not clear precisely what this refers to. Possibly it has in mind the exile brought about in 597 B.C., perhaps even, in this context, the exile of many from northern Israel in 722 B.C.

8. *I made widows among them:* a reference to women being *made widows* through the death of their husbands in war.

9. *The mother of seven sons grew faint:* a reference to the wiping out in battle of the entire male offspring of households. *her light was quenched while it was yet day:* a further reference to the loss of sons in battle, thus leaving households with no future heirs. *

Confessions and addresses

FURTHER LAMENTS BY JEREMIAH

Alas, alas, my mother, that you ever gave me birth! 10
a man doomed to strife, with the whole world
        against me.
I have borrowed from no one, I have lent to no one,
        yet all men abuse me.

The LORD answered,   11

        But I will greatly strengthen you;
        in time of distress and in time of disaster
        I will bring the enemy to your feet.

137

12   Can iron break steel from the north?[a]
15   LORD, thou knowest;
          remember me, LORD, and come to visit me,
          take vengeance for me on my persecutors.
          Be patient with me and take me not away,
        see what reproaches I endure for thy sake.
16   I have to suffer those who despise thy words,[b]
        but thy word is joy and happiness to me,
            for thou hast named me thine,
              O LORD, God of Hosts.
17   I have never kept company with any gang of
                roisterers,
              or made merry with them;
            because I felt thy hand upon me I have sat alone;
              for thou hast filled me with indignation.
18   Why then is my pain unending,
        my wound desperate and incurable?
        Thou art to me like a brook that is not to be trusted,
            whose waters fail.

19 This was the LORD's answer:

          If you will turn back to me, I will take you back
              and you shall stand before me.
          If you choose noble utterance and reject the base,
              you shall be my spokesman.

[a] *Prob. rdg.; Heb. adds* and bronze. *Heb. also adds* (13) I will give away
your wealth as spoil, and your treasure for no payment, because of your
sin throughout your country. (14) I will make your enemies pass
through a land you do not know; for my anger is a blazing fire and it
shall burn for ever (*cp. 17: 3, 4*).
[b] *I have . . . words: prob. rdg., cp. Sept.; Heb.* Thy words were found
and I ate them.

138

This people will turn again to you,
　　but you will not turn to them.
To withstand them I will make you impregnable,　　20
　　a wall of bronze.
They will attack you but they will not prevail,
　　for I am with you to deliver you
　　　and save you, says the LORD;
　　I will deliver you from the wicked,　　21
　　I will rescue you from the ruthless.

* These verses comprise two separate passages which are, however, closely related in theme. They both belong to Jeremiah's 'confessions'. The first (verses 10–12) consists of an outburst by the prophet followed by a response by God assuring him of divine protection and the ultimate vindication of both himself and the message he proclaimed. The second (verses 15–21) follows more fully the form of the individual lament and consists of Jeremiah's complaint and lamentation (verses 15–18) followed by an oracle of assurance from God (verses 19–21). (Verses 13–14 are a duplicate of 17: 3–4 and are out of place in the present context. See N.E.B. footnote.)

10. *Alas, alas, my mother, that you ever gave me birth!*: this expression of deep despair is surpassed only by the poignant outburst of 20: 14–18. The theme here, as also of the ensuing lament in verses 15–18, is once again the persecution which was Jeremiah's lot at the hands of his countrymen (cp. 11: 18 – 12: 6).

12. *Can iron break steel from the north?*: it was above all Jeremiah's persistent proclamation of Judah's inevitable subjugation by Babylon as God's judgement upon its rebellion that brought him the most vehement opposition of his countrymen who regarded him as 'an enemy of the people'. But their confidence against Babylon was but self-delusion;

their will, though it be *iron*, would be no match for the might of the foe *from the north*. God's word spoken by Jeremiah would be vindicated.

15. The first four lines of this verse contain the prophet's petition and plea for deliverance from his persecutors (cp. 11: 20; 12: 3). *see what reproaches I endure for thy sake:* following a regular feature of the individual psalms of lament, Jeremiah protests his innocence and points to his past faithfulness to his prophetic mission (verses 16–17). We may compare his protestation in these verses with the words of the psalmist in Ps. 26: 3–5:

> For thy constant love is before my eyes,
>   and I live in thy truth.
> I have not sat among worthless men,
>   nor do I mix with hypocrites;
>   I hate the company of evildoers
>   and will not sit among the ungodly.

18. There follows the characteristic plaintive question together with a cry expressing the feeling of having been abandoned by God. We may compare this with the well-known cry of dereliction with which Ps. 22 begins: 'My God, my God, why hast thou forsaken me?' (cp. Mark 15: 34).

19. God's response to Jeremiah's lament begins with an implied rebuke. Through the bitterness of his experience the prophet had come close to losing sight of his divine commission and his trust in him who had commissioned him had weakened. He had almost renounced his calling. He is bidden to *turn back* to God and to renew his trust in him. ' Unshrinking obedience, rendered without hesitation or complaint, that is the condition imposed by God on those who aspire to the high dignity of his service. And the reward of service faithfully rendered is, as in the Parable of the Pounds, more service.' (Peake.) But the disobedient *people*, when they do *turn* to the prophet, will find that his intercession is withdrawn. A similar statement is made about God himself in Zech. 7: 13.

20. But with this summons to turn again to renewed service there comes also a reaffirmation of God's promise to him at his call.

21. *I will deliver you from the wicked, I will rescue you from the ruthless:* possibly a reference to Jehoiakim and his counsellors. ✳

JEREMIAH'S LIFE MIRRORS HIS MESSAGE OF
JUDGEMENT

The word of the LORD came to me: You shall not marry **16** 1, 2 a wife; you shall have neither son nor daughter in this place. For these are the words of the LORD concerning sons 3 and daughters born in this place, the mothers who bear them and the fathers who beget them in this land: When 4 men die, struck down by deadly ulcers, there shall be no wailing for them and no burial; they shall be like dung lying upon the ground. When men perish by sword or famine, their corpses shall become food for birds and for beasts.

For these are the words of the LORD: Enter no house 5 where there is a mourning-feast; do not go in to wail or to bring comfort, for I have withdrawn my peace from this people, says the LORD, my love and affection. High and 6 low shall die in this land, but there shall be no burial, no wailing for them; no one shall gash himself, or shave his head. No one shall give the mourner a portion of bread*ᵃ* 7 to console him for the dead, nor give him*ᵇ* the cup of consolation, even for his father or mother. Nor shall you 8 enter a house where there is feasting, to sit eating and drinking there. For these are the words of the LORD of 9 Hosts, the God of Israel: In your own days, in the sight of

[a] bread: *so Sept.; Heb.* to them.   [b] *So Sept.; Heb.* them.

you all, and in this very place, I will silence all sounds of
joy and gladness, and the voice of bridegroom and bride.
10   When you tell this people all these things they will ask
you, 'Why has the LORD decreed that this great disaster is
to come upon us? What wrong have we done? What sin
11 have we committed against the LORD our God?' You
shall answer, Because your forefathers forsook me, says
the LORD, and followed other gods, serving them and
bowing down to them. They forsook me and did not
12 keep my law. And you yourselves have done worse than
your forefathers; for each of you follows the promptings
of his wicked and stubborn heart instead of obeying me.
13 So I will fling you headlong out of this land into a country
unknown to you and to your forefathers; there you can
serve other gods days and night, for I will show you no
favour.

* In style and phraseology this passage points for its composition to a Deuteronomic author (see especially the comments
below on verses 10–13). At the same time there is no reason
to doubt that it preserves facts about Jeremiah's life and behaviour which, like his 'confessions', were closely related to, and
arose from, the message he proclaimed.

1. *You shall not marry a wife:* the command given to Jeremiah was the very opposite of that given to Hosea (Hos. 1: 2).
For the latter his marriage was from the outset part and parcel
of his prophetic message and the children born to him were
themselves drawn into the symbolism of his preaching.
Though Jeremiah's celibacy did not play the significant part in
his preaching as Hosea's marriage played in his, it nevertheless
betokened his conviction of the imminent cessation of all that
was normal in everyday life, his own awareness of the
impending destruction of the nation.

4. *their corpses shall become food for birds and for beasts:* cp. e.g. 7: 33. Outside this book, this gruesome curse occurs only in Deut. 28: 26.

5. *Enter no house where there is a mourning-feast:* in the gathering shadows of imminent national disaster the *mourning* for the loss of a loved one is so dwarfed as to become irrelevant; with God's withdrawal of his peace from his people all words and deeds of *peace* are pointless. Ezekiel saw a comparable meaning in the death of his wife (Ezek. 24: 15–27).

6. *no one shall gash himself, or shave his head:* though both these mourning rites were condemned in ancient Israel as heathen practices (cp. Lev. 19: 28; Deut. 14: 1), they are mentioned here as being part of normal mourning procedures. These rites of self-mutilation and the shaving must have had a religious significance (i.e. they were not merely expressions of grief), but their origin and meaning are unknown.

7. The ritual uncleanness of the house of one who had died prevented food from being prepared there. Neighbours would bring in food and drink for the relatives of the deceased. Alternatively it is possible that the *bread* and *cup of consolation* here mentioned were given to mourners, the relatives of the deceased, on the completion of their fast.

10–13. In both form and content this passage, like 9: 12–16 (cp. 5: 19), is a Deuteronomic composition (cp. Deut. 29: 22–8; 1 Kings 9: 8–9). (For the form see the comments on 9: 10–16.) ✳

A NEW EXODUS

Therefore, says the LORD, the time is coming when men [14] shall no longer swear, 'By the life of the LORD who brought the Israelites up from Egypt', but, 'By the life of the [15] LORD who brought the Israelites back from a northern land and from all the lands to which he had dispersed them'; and I will bring them back to the soil which I gave to their forefathers.

✣ This short passage clearly presupposes the exile and is a promise that God would restore his exiled people to their homeland, bringing them forth from Babylon in a new exodus which would surpass the ancient exodus from Egypt. This promise of a new exodus is one of the dominant themes of the preaching of the anonymous prophet of the exilic period (usually referred to as Deutero-Isaiah) whose oracles are contained in Isa. 40–55 (cp. especially Isa. 43: 16–20; 48: 20f.; 51: 9–11). These two verses were composed by a Deuteronomic author and have a more appropriate context in 23: 7–8. They were no doubt inserted into ch. 16 to modify the severity of the preceding description of judgement. ✣

A FURTHER SAYING OF JUDGEMENT

16 I will send for many fishermen, says the LORD, and they shall fish for them. After that I will send for many hunters, and they shall hunt them out from every mountain and
17 hill and from the crevices in the rocks. For my eyes are on all their ways; they are not hidden from my sight, nor
18 is their wrongdoing concealed from me. I will first make them pay in full[a] for the wrong they have done and the sin they have committed by defiling with the dead lumber of their idols the land which belongs to me, and by filling it with their abominations.

✣ The announcement of judgement in verses 1–13 is continued in this passage and with equal intensity and severity.

16. *I will send for many fishermen:* for similar imagery cp. Ezek. 12: 13; 29: 4–5; Amos 4: 2; Hab. 1: 14–17. *After that I will send for many hunters:* this should not be understood as referring to a second period of destruction. Both metaphors, that of the *fishermen* and that of the *hunters*, combine to

[a] in full: *or* double.

Confessions and addresses — JER. 16: 19–21

announce both the severity and the totality of the judgement. *and they shall hunt them out from every mountain and hill and from the crevices in the rocks:* a picture of thorough and complete judgement such as is also found in Amos 9: 1–4.

18. *I will first make them pay in full:* the word *first*, which is not found in the Septuagint, may have been inserted by an editor who sought to indicate, possibly because of the preceding promise of restoration, that the judgement announced in this passage would be followed by renewal. The words *pay in full* (or 'double', see N.E.B. footnote) recall Isa. 40: 2: 'double measure for all her sins'. *by defiling with the dead lumber of their idols the land which belongs to me:* the idol gods worshipped throughout the land are ridiculed as *dead lumber*, mere 'corpses' which defile *the land* (cp. Lev. 26: 30). *

THE CONVERSION OF THE NATIONS

O LORD, my strength and my stronghold,　　　19
　my refuge in time of trouble,
to thee shall the nations come
　from the ends of the earth and say,
Our forefathers inherited only a sham,
　an idol vain and useless.
Can man make gods for himself?　　　20
　They would be no gods.
Therefore I am teaching them,　　　21
once for all will I teach them
　my power and my might,
and they shall learn that my name is the LORD.

* Ch. 16 concludes with this short poem declaring the future conversion of the nations to the worship of Israel's God Yahweh. It comes somewhat abruptly after the preceding material in this chapter and its insertion was probably promp-

145

ted by the reference in verse 18 to the idols worshipped by
Israel (cp. verse 20). Its abrupt appearance here together with
the 'universalism' it announces have led some commentators
to regard it as a later insertion into the book by an editor who
may have been influenced by the preaching of Deutero-
Isaiah (cp. especially Isa. 45: 20–4). Others, however, believe
it to be from Jeremiah, pointing to links between its phraseology and other sayings of his and to the presence of similar
statements concerning the turning of the nations to Yahweh
in some psalms from the period before the time of Jeremiah
(e.g. Ps. 2).

19. *to thee shall the nations come:* cp. 4: 2. *Our forefathers
inherited only a sham, an idol vain and useless:* the terminology
here is similar to 2: 5, 8.

20. *Can man make gods for himself?:* cp. 2: 27. *They would
be no gods:* cp. 2: 11; 5: 7. The theme of universal response is
accompanied by a familiar stress on the unreality of all other
gods. ✶

JUDAH'S INDELIBLE SIN

17 The sin of Judah is recorded with an iron tool, engraved
on the tablet of their heart with a point of adamant and
2 carved on the horns of their*a* altars to bear witness against
them.*b* Their altars and their sacred poles stand by every
3 spreading tree, on the heights and the hills in the mountain
country. I will give away your wealth as spoil, and all your
treasure for no payment,*c* because of your*d* sin throughout
4 your country. You will lose possession*e* of the patrimony which I gave you. I will make you serve your

[a] *So some MSS.; others* your.
[b] to bear...them: *prob. rdg.; Heb.* as their sons remember.
[c] for no payment: *prob. rdg., cp. 15: 13; Heb.* your hill-shrines.
[d] your: *prob. rdg., cp. 15: 13; Heb. om.*
[e] You...possession: *prob. rdg.; Heb. obscure.*

enemies as slaves in a land you do not know; for my anger is a blazing fire*ᵃ* and it shall burn for ever.

✻ 1. Judah's sin is deeply ingrained. Like an inscription carved into a rock face *with an iron tool*, it cannot be erased but is there for all to see. It goes to the core of the nation's life so that it reveals itself with an almost natural spontaneity (cp. 13 : 23). In the greatest promise for the future in the book of Jeremiah it is proclaimed that God would write his law upon his people's heart so that no longer rebellion but obedience to him would characterize the nation's life (31 : 31–4). *carved on the horns of their altars:* it has been suggested that this should be understood in connection with an act of atonement involving the sacrifice of an animal, a young bull, some of the blood of which was smeared *on the horns* (the corners) *of the altar* (cp. Lev. 4–5). If this is so the point of this allusion to *the horns* of the *altars* may be that so deep-seated was the nation's sin that it became engraved on the very *horns* of the *altars* where the blood of the sin-offering, which was supposed to wipe away sin, was smeared.

2. Yet another reference to the prevalent worship of Baal throughout the land. The *sacred poles* (Hebrew *'asherim*) were cultic objects connected with the worship of the goddess Asherah, though their precise shape as well as the function they had in that cult are unknown.

3–4. For all its iniquity the nation will be robbed of its *wealth* and treasures and will be cast out of the land into exile. These verses appear to be in place here (cp. note on 15 : 13f.). ✻

THE WAY OF LIFE

These are the words of the LORD:

5

> A curse on the man who trusts in man
>   and leans for support on human kind,
>   while his heart is far from the LORD !

[a] for…fire: *prob. rdg., cp. 15: 14; Heb.* for you have kindled a fire in my anger.

6   He shall be like a juniper*ᵃ* in the desert;
          when good comes he shall not see it.
          He shall dwell among the rocks in the wilderness,
          in a salt land where no man can live.

7   Blessed is the man who trusts in the LORD,
          and rests his confidence upon him.

8   He shall be like a tree planted by the waterside,
          that stretches its roots along the stream.
      When the heat comes it has nothing to fear;
          its spreading foliage stays green.
      In a year of drought it feels no care,
          and does not cease to bear fruit.

✻ Ch. 17 is such a mixed collection of separate and unrelated passages that we need not be surprised to find this poem amongst them. It contrasts the fate of *the man who trusts in man* with *the man* who places *his confidence* in God alone. It is strikingly similar to Ps. 1 and it is possible that one has been influenced by the other, though which is the earlier is impossible to say. Almost certainly this passage does not come from Jeremiah. Its straightforward belief that the just prosper whilst evil men suffer retribution was belied by the prophet's own bitter experiences (cp. especially 12: 1f.). ✻

FURTHER SAYINGS ON REWARD AND RETRIBUTION

9   The heart is the most deceitful of all things,
      desperately sick;*ᵇ* who can fathom it?

10   I, the LORD, search the mind
          and test the heart,
        requiting man for his conduct,
          and as his deeds deserve.

[a] *Mng. of Heb. word uncertain.*
[b] the most...sick: *or* too deceitful for any man.

Like a partridge which gathers into its nest   11
eggs which it has not laid,
so is the man who amasses wealth unjustly.
Before his days are half done he must leave it,
and prove but a fool at the last.

✳ Attached to the preceding poem are two short sayings
centring on much the same theme. The first (verses 9–10)
begins with a proverb concerning the innate selfishness and
deceitfulness of the human *heart* and concludes with a statement that God knows the secrets of the *heart* and rewards
each *man* according to his *deeds*, good or bad. The second (verse
11) also reads rather like a saying such as we might expect to
find in the book of Proverbs. The man who acquires riches
unjustly is compared with a bird which hatches out *eggs* which
are not its own. When the young birds grow up they quickly
desert her, instinctively recognizing her as a different breed.
So also ill-gotten riches are ephemeral; soon they are gone and
he who strove dishonestly to acquire them is left worse off
than ever, *but a fool at the last*. The book of Proverbs has much
to say about the *fool* in society. The evidence suggests that
these two sayings together with verses 5–8 derive from teachers
of wisdom in ancient Israel such as those from whom we have
received the book of Proverbs. ✳

THE HOPE OF ISRAEL

O throne of glory, exalted from the beginning,   12
the place of our sanctuary,
O LORD on whom Israel's hope is fixed,   13
all who reject thee shall be put to shame;
all in this land who forsake thee shall be humbled,*a*
for they have rejected the fountain of living water.*b*

[*a*] humbled: *prob. rdg.; Heb.* written.
[*b*] *Prob. rdg.; Heb. adds* the LORD.

✶ Though sometimes regarded as two separate sayings, these verses are best understood together.

12. *O throne of glory:* since the temple, more specifically the 'holy of holies', was where God was believed to be enthroned above the sacred Ark (cp. e.g. Ps. 80: 1), to address the *throne of glory* was of course to address God himself. Some commentators argue that Jeremiah could not have composed such a saying as this on the grounds that the attitude towards the temple here expressed is at variance with his own attitude towards it (cp. 7: 1–15). But we must not confuse the prophet's condemnation of the people's blasphemous distortion of the belief in God's presence in the temple with that belief in itself. There is no evidence that Jeremiah rejected the ancient belief that the temple was the holy dwelling-place of God. What he demanded was that the people amongst whom God dwelt in his holiness should themselves be holy and obedient.

13. For some of the phraseology in this verse cp. 2: 13 and 14: 8. The N.E.B. reading *humbled* is preferable to the Hebrew text which reads 'written' and makes little sense. ✶

A FURTHER LAMENT

14   Heal me, O Lord, and I shall be healed,
      save me and I shall be saved;
        for thou art my praise.

15   They say to me, 'Where is the word of the Lord?
      Let it come if it can!'

16   It is not the thought of disaster that makes me press
        after thee;
      never did I desire this day of despair.
      Thou knowest all that has passed my lips;
        it was approved by thee.

17   Do not become a terror to me;
      thou art my only refuge on the day of disaster.

May my persecutors be foiled, not I;   18
may they be terrified, not I.
Bring on them the day of disaster;
destroy them, destroy them utterly.

✷ This passage is yet another of Jeremiah's 'confessions' composed in the form of an individual psalm of lament (see p. 112).

14. Like many individual psalms of lament this lament by Jeremiah begins with a petition coupled with an expression of confidence in, or ascription of praise to, God (cp. e.g. Ps. 4: 1).

15. *They say to me, 'Where is the word of the LORD? Let it come if it can!'*: if at times God's *word* was 'joy and happiness' to Jeremiah (cp. 15: 16), at other times it gave rise to a crisis of faith for him, so much so that he even wished at moments to abandon his ministry (cp. 20: 9). The lack of confirmation of his message and the ridicule to which this exposed him filled him with deep despair.

16. *It is not the thought of disaster that makes me press after thee*: he had been dismissed as a prophet of evil, as one who appeared in the eyes of his countrymen actually to wish *disaster* upon the nation. He protested his innocence of such a charge. But it was a charge which he had to live with and coupled with his own inner doubts and turmoil it was a burden not easily borne.

18. See the comment on 11: 20. ✷

ON KEEPING THE SABBATH

These were the words of the LORD to me: Go and stand   19
in the Benjamin[a] Gate, through which the kings of Judah
go in and out, and in all the gates of Jerusalem. Say, Hear   20
the words of the LORD, you princes of Judah, all you men
of Judah, and all you inhabitants of Jerusalem who come

[a] Benjamin: *prob. rdg.; Heb.* sons of the people.

21 in through these gates. These are the words of the LORD: Observe this with care, that you do not carry any load on the sabbath or bring it through the gates of Jerusalem.
22 You shall not bring any load out of your houses or do any work on the sabbath, but you shall keep the sabbath day
23 holy as I commanded your forefathers. Yet they did not obey or pay attention, but obstinately refused to hear or
24 learn their lesson. Now if you will obey me, says the LORD, and refrain from bringing any load through the gates of this city on the sabbath, and keep that day holy by doing
25 no work on it, then kings shall come through the gates of this city, kings*a* who shall sit on David's throne. They shall come riding in chariots or on horseback, escorted by their captains, by the men of Judah and the inhabitants of
26 Jerusalem; and this city shall be inhabited for ever. People shall come from the cities of Judah, the country round Jerusalem, the land of Benjamin, the Shephelah, the hill-country and the Negeb, bringing whole-offerings, sacrifices, grain-offerings, and frankincense, bringing also
27 thank-offerings to the house of the LORD. But if you do not obey me by keeping the sabbath day holy and by not carrying any load as you come through the gates of Jerusalem on the sabbath, then I will set fire to those gates; it shall consume the palaces of Jerusalem and shall not be put out.

* This is another passage composed in the characteristic style and phraseology of the prose material throughout the book. In nature and form it belongs to a series of 'sermons' in the book which are concerned with the nation's obedi-ence to God's law. Whereas the 'sermons' in 7: 1–15 and

[a] *Prob. rdg.; Heb. adds* and officers.

11: 1–17 are concerned with a general call to obedience to
the law, this 'sermon', like that in 34: 8–22, singles out a
specific law for particular emphasis, the law commanding
observance of the sabbath day. The form of this 'sermon' is
closely akin to that of the other sermons concerned with the
same basic theme. After an introduction it has a proclamation
of the law followed by a promise of blessing for obedience to
it and a threat of judgement for disobedience.

19. *the Benjamin Gate:* cp. 37: 13; 38: 7. This *Gate* was
probably in the north wall of the city and was possibly, though
not certainly, so called simply because it led to the territory
of the tribe of *Benjamin*. The N.E.B. takes the reading in the
Hebrew text 'the sons of the people' to be a corruption of
'Benjamin'. A gate designated 'the gate of the sons of the
people' is nowhere else attested.

21. *Observe this with care, that you do not carry any load on the
sabbath:* the law commanding observance of *the sabbath* was
not new in Jeremiah's day. It was already contained in the
Decalogue (Exod. 20: 8–11; Deut. 5: 12–15). That Jeremiah
may have had something to say about keeping *the sabbath* is
therefore possible. But the emphasis on *the sabbath* exemplified
in the present passage according to which the nation's very
existence is conditional upon observance of it can scarcely
have come from Jeremiah but is best understood as reflecting
the more intense significance and importance attached to *the
sabbath* which appears to have emerged among the exiles in
Babylon to become one of the dominant characteristics of post-
exilic Judaism. With the command here prohibiting the carrying of burdens on *the sabbath* we may compare Neh. 13: 15–22.

22. *or do any work on the sabbath:* some of the terminology
of *the sabbath* law as formulated in the Decalogue is also present
in this passage. The command not to *do any work on the sabbath*
is found in Exod. 20: 9–10 and Deut. 5: 13–14, whilst the
command to *keep the sabbath day holy* is found in Exod. 20: 8,
11 and Deut. 5: 12.

25–6. These verses set out the blessings which will be

bestowed upon the nation if it observes the sabbath. The security of the state will be guaranteed, whilst the people from all over *the country* – from the territory *round Jerusalem*, from the *land* to the north of it (*Benjamin*), to the east of it (*the Shephelah*), as well as to the south of it (*the Negeb*) – will flock to *Jerusalem* to bring their offerings to God in his holy temple.

27. But failure to observe *the sabbath* will incur the destruction of *Jerusalem* as God's judgement upon the nation's disobedience to *the sabbath* law. If, as its style, form and content indicate, this 'sermon' was composed by Deuteronomic authors living in the period of the exile, those to whom it was addressed would have been reminded of their fathers' disobedience to this law of God and at the same time would have been exhorted by it to renewed obedience to *the sabbath* law. ✻

THE PARABLE OF THE POTTER'S VESSEL

18 These are the words which came to Jeremiah from the
2 LORD: Go down at once to the potter's house, and there I
3 will tell you what I have to say. So I went down to the
4 potter's house and found him working at the wheel. Now and then a vessel he was making out of the clay would be spoilt in his hands, and then he would start again and
5 mould it into another vessel to his liking. Then the word
6 of the LORD came to me: Can I not deal with you, Israel, says the LORD, as the potter deals with his clay? You are
7 clay in my hands like the clay in his, O house of Israel. At any moment I may threaten to uproot a nation or a king-
8 dom, to pull it down and destroy it. But if the nation which I have threatened turns back from its wicked ways, then I shall think better of the evil I had in mind to bring
9 on it. Or at any moment I may decide to build or to plant
10 a nation or a kingdom. But if it does evil in my sight and

does not obey me, I shall think better of the good I had
in mind for it. Go now and tell the men of Judah and the 11
inhabitants of Jerusalem that these are the words of the
LORD: I am the potter; I am preparing evil for you and
perfecting my designs against you. Turn back, every one
of you, from his evil course; mend your ways and your
doings. But they answer, 'Things are past hope. We will 12
do as we like, and each of us will follow the promptings
of his own wicked and stubborn heart.'

* Though based upon a saying of Jeremiah, this passage as it
now stands is the work of a Deuteronomic author. Verses 7–12
are composed in the characteristic style of the prose throughout the book and verses 1–6 alone look like the original
saying of the prophet. The message of this original saying was
one of judgement and renewal after judgement, a theme which
is found frequently elsewhere in the book. As a potter re-
moulds a spoilt vessel on his wheel, so God would remould
his people who had been 'spoilt' by their sinfulness; he would
destroy what they had been and reconstitute them to conform
to the original purpose he intended for them. In verses 7–10
the idea of God's sovereign control over Israel is extended to
the nations in general; they too are as clay in his hands and
their life and destiny are ordered by him alone. Verse 11
directs attention to Judah and Jerusalem: because of their sinfulness they have forfeited God's good purposes for them. As
a result, like any other nation which rebels against God, they
stand under judgement unless they turn back to him. Verse
12 records that they refused to repent. By these means the
author of verses 7–12 orientated the message of the original
saying in verses 1–6 towards judgement alone (cp. especially
verse 11).

2. The making of pottery must have been one of the most
stable, not to say lucrative, trades in ancient Israel. To judge
from the vast quantities of broken pottery which are unearthed

in archaeological digs of ancient sites, it was in plentiful supply
and when broken was easily replaced. It is largely because of
these finds of pottery that archaeologists are able to date the
various layers of sites they are examining, for the ware and
shape as well as the designs of pottery varied from period to
period and so afford an indication of the particular time in
Israel's history they were in use. Another saying of Jeremiah
involving pottery is recorded in ch. 19.

3. *the wheel:* the Hebrew word for this suggests that there
were two wheels (the word in Hebrew is what is known as a
'dual'). Probably there was a small *wheel* on which the clay
was placed and below this small wheel a larger wheel which was
spun around and by its weight gave the necessary momentum.
We do not know of any apparatus employed for spinning the
wheel. Most probably it was done by an assistant.

7. On the terminology of uprooting, pulling down and
destroying here and the terminology of building and planting
in verse 9, see the commentary on 1: 10. ✳

ISRAEL'S UNNATURAL BEHAVIOUR

13 Therefore these are the words of the LORD:

Inquire among the nations: who ever heard the like
    of this?
The virgin Israel has done a thing most horrible.
14 Will the snow cease to fall on the rocky slopes of
    Lebanon?
Will the cool rain streaming in torrents ever fail[a]?
15 No, but my people have forgotten me;
    they burn sacrifices to a mere idol,
    so they stumble in their paths, the ancient ways,
    and they take to byways and unmade roads;

[a] fail: *prob. rdg., cp. Sept.; Heb.* be uprooted.

their own land they lay waste,   16
and men will jeer at it for ever in contempt.
All who go by will be horror-struck and shake their
    heads.
    Like a wind from the east   17
I will scatter them before their enemies.
    In the hour of their downfall
I will turn my back towards them and not my face.

✻ Jeremiah contrasts the unnaturalness of Israel's sin against
God with the constancy of nature. In thought the passage may
be compared with 2: 10–13.

14. The contrast here drawn may be compared with 8: 7.

15. *they burn sacrifices to a mere idol:* literally, 'they burn
sacrifices to what is worthless'. A good paraphrase which
catches the meaning of it as a reference to Israel's worship of
Baal is 'To the Fraud they burn offerings.' *so they stumble in
their paths, the ancient ways:* that is, the 'way' laid down for
them by Yahweh, the laws set forth from ancient times for the
ordering of the nation's life as his holy people. *they take to
byways and unmade roads:* they follow the 'way' of the
Canaanite cults, their life both with regard to the cult and
social behaviour being governed by their worship of Baal and
other gods of Canaanite religion.

16. They thus bring disaster upon themselves, the judgement of their evil ways. ✻

JEREMIAH CURSES HIS ADVERSARIES

'Come, let us decide what to do with Jeremiah', men 18
say. 'There will still be priests to guide us, still wise men
to advise, still prophets to proclaim the word. Come, let
us invent some charges against him; let us pay no attention
to his message.'

19   But do thou, O LORD, pay attention,
            and hear what my opponents are saying against
            me.
20   Is good to be repaid with evil?[a]
        Remember how I stood before thee,
        pleading on their behalf
        to avert thy wrath from them.
21   Therefore give their sons over to famine,
            leave them at the mercy of the sword.
        Let their women be childless and widowed,
            let death carry off their men,
        let their young men be cut down in battle.
22   Bring raiders upon them without warning,
            and let screams of terror ring out from their houses.
        For they have dug a pit to catch me
        and have hidden snares for my feet.
23   Well thou knowest, O LORD,
        all their murderous plots against me.
            Do not blot out their wrongdoing
            or annul their sin;
            when they are brought stumbling into thy presence,
            deal with them on the day of thy anger.

✶ This passage comprises yet another of Jeremiah's 'confessions' (verses 19–23) the background to which is briefly narrated in verse 18.

18. As in the case of the 'confessions' recorded in 11: 18–20, 12: 1–6 and 15: 10–18, the occasion for this further lament is a plot to silence the prophet. '*There will still be priests to guide us, still wise men to advise, still prophets to proclaim the word.*' (more literally 'instruction shall not perish from the priest, nor

[a] *Prob. rdg.; Heb. adds* they have dug a pit for me (*cp. verse 22*).

counsel from the wise, nor the word from the prophet').
Jeremiah had been relentless in his condemnation of the three
classes of official functionaries here mentioned (cp. e.g. 6:
13–15; 23: 9–40) and it may be inferred that the plot against
him was in this instance instigated by a group of them.

let us pay no attention to his message: the Septuagint omits the
negative, thus reading 'let us pay attention to his message (lit.
his words)'. It is possible that this preserves the original text,
the meaning being that those who desired to silence the
prophet would gather evidence from his utterances with which
to bring charges against him.

20. *Is good to be repaid with evil?:* much the same question as
in 12: 1 and prompted by the same sort of experience in the
prophet's life reflected there. *Remember how I stood before thee,
pleading on their behalf:* a reference to Jeremiah's intercessory
role on *behalf* of the people. We may compare what is here
said with the prophet's protestation in 17: 16.

21–3. The vengeance here prayed for by Jeremiah against
his enemies is quite unparalleled in both vehemence and
length in any of the other confessions. Some commentators
have argued that such bitter outcries for vengeance were no
part of Jeremiah's original laments but have been inserted by
later scribes. But the cry for vengeance is too constant a
feature of these passages to be so easily removed. To us they
may seem unworthy of Jeremiah. But few men rise completely above the spirit of their times and Jeremiah, though he
reached heights of spiritual experience, also plumbed the
depths of human despair and anguish. In the end there is more
to be gained from accepting and seeking to understand his
bitter and passionate outbursts for vengeance than by a facile
expurgation of the passages in question. We need also to
realize how closely the prophet felt himself to be delivering
not only his own message but God's; cp. 'they have not
rejected you, it is I whom they have rejected' (1 Sam. 8: 7). *

A SYMBOLIC ACTION

19 These are the words of the LORD: Go and buy an earthenware jar. Then take with you[a] some of the elders of
2 the people and of the priests, and go out to the Valley of Ben-hinnom, on which the Gate of the Potsherds opens,
3 and there proclaim what I tell you. Say, Hear the word of the LORD, you princes of Judah and inhabitants of Jerusalem. These are the words of the LORD of Hosts the God of Israel: I will bring on this place a disaster which shall
4 ring in the ears of all who hear of it. For they have forsaken me, and treated this place as if it were not mine, burning sacrifices to other gods whom neither they nor their fathers nor the kings of Judah have known, and
5 filling this place with the blood of the innocent. They have built shrines to Baal, where they burn their sons as whole-offerings to Baal. It was no command of mine;
6 I never spoke of it; it never entered my thought. Therefore, says the LORD, the time is coming when this place shall no longer be called Topheth or the Valley of Ben-
7 hinnom, but the Valley of Slaughter. In this place I will shatter the plans of Judah and Jerusalem as a jar is shattered; I will make the people fall by the sword before their enemies, at the hands of those who would kill them, and I will give their corpses to the birds and beasts to devour.
8 I will make this city a scene of horror and contempt, so that every passer-by will be horror-struck and jeer in
9 contempt at the sight of its wounds. I will compel men to eat the flesh of their sons and their daughters; they shall devour one another's flesh in the dire straits to which their

[a] Then...you: *so Pesh.; Heb. om.*

enemies and those who would kill them will reduce them
in the siege. Then you must shatter the jar before the eyes 10
of the men who have come with you and say to them, 11
These are the words of the LORD of Hosts: Thus will I
shatter this people and this city as one shatters an earthen
vessel so that it cannot be mended, and the dead shall be
buried in Topheth because there is no room elsewhere to
bury them. This is what I will do to this place, says the 12
LORD, and to those who live there: I will make this city
like Topheth. Because of their defilement, the houses of 13
Jerusalem and those of the kings of Judah shall be like
Topheth, every one of the houses on whose roofs men
have burnt sacrifices to the host of heaven and poured
drink-offerings to other gods.

Jeremiah came in from Topheth, where the LORD had 14
sent him to prophesy, and stood in the court of the LORD's
house. He said to all the people, These are the words of 15
the LORD of Hosts the God of Israel: I am bringing on this
city and on all its blood-spattered altars every disaster
with which I have threatened it, for its people have remained obstinate and refused to listen to me.

When Pashhur son of Immer the priest, the chief officer **20**
in the house of the LORD, heard Jeremiah prophesying
these things, he had him flogged*a* and put him into the 2
stocks at the Upper Gate of Benjamin, in the house of the
LORD. The next morning he released him, and Jeremiah 3
said to him, The LORD has called you not Pashhur but
Magor-missabib.*b* For these are the words of the LORD: 4
I will make you a terror to yourself and to all your friends;
they shall fall by the sword of the enemy before your very

[*a*] had him flogged: *or* struck him.   [*b*] *That is* Terror let loose.

eyes. I will hand over all Judah to the king of Babylon,
and he will deport them to Babylon and put them to the
5 sword. I will give all this city's store of wealth and riches
and all the treasures of the kings of Judah to their enemies;
they shall seize them as spoil and carry them off to Baby-
6 lon. You, Pashhur, and all your household shall go into
captivity and come to Babylon. There shall you die and
there shall you be buried, you and all your friends to
whom you have been a false prophet.

* At first glance this narrative reads quite straightforwardly.
Jeremiah is commanded by God to take 'an earthenware jar'
and to go to the 'Valley of Ben-hinnom' bringing with him
some 'elders' and 'priests' who are to witness what he is to
say and do there. In the appointed place Jeremiah announces
the judgement which God is about to inflict upon 'Judah' and
'Jerusalem' and at the same time smashes 'the jar' to symbolize that judgement. Subsequently he returns to the city and
there repeats this declaration of judgement. At this point he is
arrested by 'Pashhur son of Immer' and placed in 'the stocks'.
He is released the following morning and announces judgement against Pashhur himself.

However, a closer reading of the narrative reveals a certain
amount of confusion. Thus although in verse 1 Jeremiah is
told to take with him some 'elders' and 'priests', verses 3–9
are an address directed not to these but to the 'princes of
Judah' and the 'inhabitants of Jerusalem': it is not until verses
10–11*a* that the symbolic action involving the smashing of
'the jar' in the presence of the men who accompanied
Jeremiah is recorded. Furthermore, there is a difference in
content between verses 1–2, 10–11*a* and verses 3–9 with which
we must also associate verses 11*b*–13 which also refer to
'Topheth'. In verses 1–2, 10–11*a* the judgement announced by
the prophet is symbolized by the smashing of 'the jar'; in

verses 3–9, 11*b*–13, however, the emphasis is on 'Topheth', 'the Valley of Ben-hinnom', which is to be the place where 'Judah and Jerusalem' are to be destroyed (verse 6), where those who perish in the coming destruction will be buried for lack of 'room elsewhere' (verse 11), or which as a place of death and destruction is evoked as an illustration of what Jerusalem will be like as a result of the imminent disaster (verse 12).

For these reasons we must probably regard verses 1–13 as embodying an original account of the symbolic action involving the 'earthenware jar' which has been expanded by an editor, or perhaps a conflation of two separate incidents, the one concerning the symbolic action and the other 'the Valley of Ben-hinnom'. Of these two possibilities the former is the more likely, for verses 3–9 are very strongly Deuteronomic in style and phraseology and have thus all the appearance of having been inserted here by a Deuteronomic author (see also below under verse 7).

1–2. If we regard the material concerning *the Valley of Ben-hinnom* in verses 3–9, 11*b*–13 as editorial, it is probable that we should regard the command to Jeremiah recorded in verses 1–2 as having originally referred only to *the Gate of the Potsherds*. The location of this gate in ancient Jerusalem is unknown. It has been suggested that it acquired its name because it was near a dump where potters, whose workshops were possibly in the Hinnom Valley, discarded broken or defective pottery. To identify the Hinnom Valley as that *on which the Gate of the Potsherds opens* is quite superfluous; that *Valley* scarcely needed any such identification! We should therefore take the reference to *the Valley of Ben-hinnom* as editorial and understand the original command to have been: *Go and buy an earthenware jar. Then take with you some of the elders of the people and of the priests, and go . . . to . . . the Gate of the Potsherds.* That gate would obviously have been an apt place at which to perform the symbolic action described in verses 10f. *an earthenware jar:* the Hebrew word here translated was the name of a narrow-necked bottle or decanter and was derived from a verb meaning 'to make a gurgling noise', obviously because of the sound the water made when poured from this particular kind of vessel. *the Valley of Ben-hinnom:* on this see on 2: 23.

3. *this place:* that is, Jerusalem. *I will bring on this place a disaster which shall ring in the ears of all who hear of it:* this expression is found almost verbatim in 2 Kings 21: 12, a Deuteronomic passage.

4. *other gods whom neither they nor their fathers nor the kings of Judah have known:* cp. Deut. 13: 6; 28: 64.

5. *where they burn their sons as whole-offerings to Baal:* on the human sacrifice at Topheth see the comments on 7: 31.

7. *In this place I will shatter the plans of Judah and Jerusalem as a jar is shattered:* the Hebrew word here translated *I will shatter* is from the same verb as the word for *earthenware jar* in verse 1. The N.E.B. correctly sees the use of this verb in verse 7 as intended as a play upon the word in verse 1 and so translates it *I will shatter...as a jar is shattered.* Incidentally we may note that the use of this verb here supports the view that verses 3–9 did not originally have a separate existence but originated as an expansion of the account of the symbolic act with the earthenware *jar* in verses 1–2, 10–11*a. and I will give their corpses to the birds and beasts to devour:* we have already come across this expression in 7: 33 and 16: 4 (both prose passages) and have noted that outside the book of Jeremiah it occurs only in Deut. 28: 26. Its presence here is further evidence that this chapter owes its present form to a Deuteronomic editor.

9. In both phraseology and content this verse is strikingly similar to Deut. 28: 53. The expression *in the dire straits to which their enemies and those who would kill them will reduce them in the siege* occurs elsewhere only in Deut. 28: 53, 55, 57.

10. *Then you must shatter the jar before the eyes of the men who have come with you:* this together with what follows up to 'mended' in verse 11 is the obvious continuation of verses 1–2

and embodies the original symbolic act and the saying of Jeremiah which an editor has greatly expanded in this chapter.

There are many examples of symbolic actions performed by prophets in ancient Israel, and we have already seen the symbol of the girdle (13: 1–11) and of Jeremiah's celibacy (16: 1–13). In 1 Kings 22: 11 it is recorded that the prophet Zedekiah son of Kenaanah made for himself horns of iron and declared to Ahab and Jehoshaphat: 'With horns like these you shall gore the Aramaeans and make an end of them.' Similarly, Elisha told Jehoash king of Israel to shoot arrows in the direction of Syria, thus symbolizing Israel's forthcoming victory over the Aramaeans (2 Kings 13: 14–19). Or again, Hosea's marriage to Gomer was a symbolic enactment of Israel's relationship to God, just as the names he gave his children symbolized God's judgement upon his unfaithful 'wife' Israel (Hos. 1–2). Isaiah likewise performed symbolic actions by the names he gave his children (Shear-jashub 7: 3; Maher-shalal-hash-baz 8: 1; possibly also Immanuel 7: 14). Symbolic actions were profusely employed by Ezekiel; several such symbols appear in Ezek. 4–5 and among others in the book the symbol portraying the union of Israel and Judah in 37: 15–20 is a good example. Notwithstanding the name we give to these actions, it is a mistake to conceive of them as merely illustrations or 'visual aids'. Rather, like the word of God spoken by a prophet, these symbolic actions had an effective power. That is, they were believed actually to set in motion the event, whether good or evil, which they symbolized. Thus when Jeremiah smashed the earthenware *jar* his action was believed to have set in motion the judgement which it symbolized. An excellent example of the prophetic use of a symbolic action is provided in chs. 27–8 where Jeremiah's symbolic enactment by means of an ox-yoke of the nation's subjugation by the Babylonians is countered by the prophet Hananiah who breaks the ox-yoke thus rendering powerless, as it would have been believed, Jeremiah's action and declaration of judgement and at the same time replacing it by a new symbolic action announcing the imminent breaking of Babylonian dominion by God. Hananiah's action was in turn countered by Jeremiah who subsequently replaced the wooden yoke, which had been broken by Hananiah, by an iron yoke, thus confirming and further strengthening his initial symbolic action.

11. *and the dead shall be buried in Topheth:* the meaning of the references to *Topheth* in verses 3–9, 11–13 varies. Here it is the place where those who perish in the coming judgement are to be buried; in verses 4–5 it is referred to as the place of the heinous practice of human sacrifice; in verses 6–7 it is referred to as the place where the imminent destruction of the sinful nation is to take place and where Judah's plans are to be shattered like a jar; in verse 12 'Topheth' as a place of death and destruction betokens what the fate of Jerusalem itself is to be.

14–15. These verses provide the link between 19: 1–13 and 20: 1–6.

14. *Jeremiah came in from Topheth:* by a slight emendation the Hebrew word for *from Topheth* can be changed to read 'from the entry' (i.e. 'from the entry of the Gate of the Potsherds'; cp. verse 2 where the Hebrew text is literally 'at the entry of the Gate of the Potsherds'). If, as seems likely, the material in verses 3–9, 11*b*–13 concerning Topheth is editorial, this suggested emendation has much to commend it.

15. *blood-spattered altars:* other English translations have here 'upon all its towns', thus understanding the text to refer to Jerusalem and its surrounding towns and villages. The N.E.B. translation understands the word here translated 'towns' to be derived rather from a word found in Ugaritic meaning 'a blood-daubed stone' (cp. note on 2: 28).

20: 1–6. More than any other prophet Jeremiah suffered considerably at the hands of his fellow-countrymen because of the message he proclaimed (cp. also 11: 21–3; 26; 37–8).

1. *Pashhur son of Immer:* two officials bearing the name *Pashhur* are referred to in the book of Jeremiah, the one mentioned here who is probably also to be identified with the

father of Gedaliah in 38: 1, and the other 'Pashhur son of Malchiah' referred to in 21: 1 and 38: 1. The name *Pashhur* is of Egyptian origin. *the chief officer in the house of the LORD:* his function was evidently to keep order in the temple and its precincts and to deal with any trouble-makers. It was possibly because of orders given by *Pashhur* that Jeremiah was banned from entering the temple on the famous occasion described in ch. 36 and had to send his scribe Baruch instead to read the scroll of the prophet's oracles. See also below under verse 6.

2. *Upper Gate of Benjamin:* not to be confused with the Benjamin Gate mentioned in 37: 13; 38: 7 which was a city gate. The gate here referred to was one of those which led into the temple precincts and is probably to be identified with the 'upper gate of the house of the LORD' built by Jotham (2 Kings 15: 35; cp. Ezek. 9: 2). From its name we can deduce that it was on the north side of the temple area, that is, facing the territory of *Benjamin*.

3. *Magor-missabib:* 'terror let loose' (see N.E.B. footnote) or 'Terror on every side', used in 6: 25 of the relentless enemy from the north. Jeremiah's naming of Pashhur in this way belongs to the category of symbolic action discussed above. It is thus wrong to think of it as nothing more than an expression of the prophet's intense animosity towards the one who had punished him. On the contrary, it was a terrible pronouncement of judgement upon *Pashhur*; the name amounted to a curse upon him, involving him in the terror to come upon Judah.

6. *You, Pashhur, and all your household shall go into captivity:* in ch. 29, which concerns matters which arose after the deportation of 597 B.C., *Pashhur*'s office is held by one Zephaniah son of Maaseiah. From this we may infer that *Pashhur* was among those who had been taken into exile in 597 B.C. *you have been a false prophet:* it is unlikely that Pashhur was a *prophet* and we must probably understand the word here to have been employed loosely to describe him as one who, as a leading figure in the temple, had led the people astray. ✻

JEREMIAH'S INNER STRUGGLE

7   O Lord, thou hast duped me, and I have been thy dupe;
        thou hast outwitted me and hast prevailed.
     I have been made a laughing-stock all the day long,
     everyone mocks me.
8   Whenever I speak I must needs cry out
     and proclaim violence and destruction.
     I am reproached and mocked all the time
     for uttering the word of the Lord.
9   Whenever I said, 'I will call him to mind no more,
     nor speak in his name again',
     then his word was imprisoned in my body,
     like a fire blazing in my heart,
     and I was weary with holding it under,
     and could endure no more.
10   For I heard many whispering,[a]
     'Denounce him! we will denounce him.'
     All my friends were on the watch for a false step,
     saying, 'Perhaps he may be tricked, then we can
            catch him
     and take our revenge.'
11   But the Lord is on my side, strong and ruthless,
     therefore my persecutors shall stumble and fall
            powerless.
     Bitter shall be their abasement when they fail,
     and their shame shall long be remembered.
12   O Lord of Hosts, thou dost test the righteous
     and search the depths of the heart;
     to thee have I committed my cause,

[a] *Prob. rdg.; Heb. adds* Terror let loose.

168

let me see thee take vengeance on them.
Sing to the LORD, praise the LORD;   13
for he rescues the poor from those who would do
     them wrong.

✻ This passage is yet another of Jeremiah's 'confessions' and, like other such poems, follows the form of an individual psalm of lament. In its present context it might appear to have arisen from the suffering he endured at the hands of Pashhur (20: 1–6), but more probably it arose from the more general background of the persecution he encountered and the on-going inner turmoil he experienced.

7. *O LORD, thou hast duped me:* no other 'confession' reveals more clearly than this one the tension that existed in Jeremiah's mind between the vocation he knew to be his and the natural re-actions of his heart to the calumny and abuse it brought him. In this his bitterest outburst against God (cp. 15: 18) he protests that he has been *duped*, enticed by God himself into a task the nature and consequences of which had been hidden from him.

8. *Whenever I speak I must needs cry out and proclaim violence and destruction:* it seems that Jeremiah's message of judgement brought him on the one hand his most severe physical per-secution and on the other bitter ridicule, presumably because the judgement he repeatedly announced was not seen to materialize. Possibly, therefore, this particular lament belongs to the earliest years of his ministry and well before the storm-clouds which finally brought disaster to the nation appeared.

9. *Whenever I said, 'I will call him to mind no more, nor speak in his name again':* his natural reaction in the face of the abuse and ridicule he encountered was to abandon his vocation and ministry. But try as he would, he could not escape the com-pulsion of God's word within him. Silence merely aggravated his plight and so 'the word of the Lord which had been an outward reproach now became an inward torture...Yahweh has brought him into a strait from which he can find neither exit nor retreat' (Skinner).

10. *All my friends were on the watch for a false step:* we can well imagine that there were not a few who desired the prophet's imprisonment if not execution. An attempt was made to convict him of blasphemy because of his speech concerning the temple, but he was acquitted (cp. ch. 26). The *friends* mentioned may be a reference to his kinsmen (cp. 12: 6).

11. An expression of confidence in deliverance by God such as is characteristic of psalms of lament.

13. This verse is sometimes regarded as a secondary addition to this poem on the grounds that it is at variance with the mood of the passage. But psalms of lament frequently contain or end with such an expression of confidence, probably prompted by an oracle of assurance not usually recorded but given by a cultic official in response to the worshipper's lament and petition (e.g. Ps. 6: 8f.). Though it would be wrong to assume that this verse presupposes such an oracle of assurance given by a cultic official to Jeremiah, it may well express an inner experience of calm and renewed confidence which came to him on this occasion. ✻

ULTIMATE DESPAIR

14   A curse on the day when I was born!
            Be it for ever unblessed,
            the day when my mother bore me!
15   A curse on the man who brought word to my father,
            'A child is born to you, a son',
            and gladdened his heart!
16   That man shall fare like the cities
            which the LORD overthrew without mercy.
            He shall hear cries of alarm in the morning
            and uproar at noon,
17   because death did not claim me before birth,
            and my mother did not become my grave,
            her womb great with me for ever.

> Why did I come forth from the womb   18
> to know only sorrow and toil,
> to end my days in shame?

✻ If, as the final verse of the lament in verses 7–13 indicates, Jeremiah at times experienced fresh confidence and peace of mind, these verses at the end of ch. 20 reveal a depth of misery and agony far surpassing any other cry of despair among the prophet's recorded lamentations. No ray of light pierces the darkness of Jeremiah's mind here; no word of comfort or relief eases the feeling of total hopelessness which has seized and overwhelmed him. The passage is unparalleled in the entire Old Testament with the exception of Job 3: 3–12 which, however, is possibly partly dependent upon it.

16. *like the cities which the LORD overthrew without mercy:* a reference to the destruction of Sodom and Gomorrah (Gen. 19; cp. Isa. 1: 9). ✻

Kings and prophets denounced

(A) THE MONARCHY: JUDGEMENT AND RENEWAL

✻ The section 21: 1 – 23: 8 comprises a number of oracles and sayings in poetry and prose, several announcing judgement against the last four kings of Judah and others directed against or concerning the monarchy in general. The theme of judgement upon the monarchy in 21: 1 – 22: 30 changes to one of hope for its future renewal and restoration under kings (23: 1–4) or an ideal king (23: 5–6) to be raised up by God to reign over his people in peace and righteousness. Verses 7–8 bring the complex as a whole to an end with a short saying announcing the future restoration of the exiles to their homeland in a new exodus which would surpass in magnitude the original exodus from Egypt.

It is clear that these sayings did not all originate at the same
time. In addition, not all of them derive from Jeremiah himself. The substantial amount of prose in the complex is an
indication that here as elsewhere in the book Deuteronomic
editors have subjected original sayings of the prophet to
further expansion and development and supplemented them
with material of their own composition. There is every
reason to believe that the complex in its present form derives
from these editors. ✲

THE INEVITABILITY OF JUDGEMENT

21 THE WORD WHICH CAME FROM THE LORD to
Jeremiah when King Zedekiah sent to him Pashhur
son of Malchiah and Zephaniah the priest, son of Maaseiah,
2 with this request: 'Nebuchadrezzar king of Babylon is
making war on us; inquire of the LORD on our behalf.
Perhaps the LORD will perform a miracle as he has done in
past times, so that Nebuchadrezzar may raise the siege.'
3, 4 But Jeremiah answered them, Tell Zedekiah, these are the
words of the LORD the God of Israel: I will turn back
upon you your own weapons with which you are
fighting the king of Babylon and the Chaldaeans besieging
you outside the wall; and I will bring them into the heart
5 of this city. I myself will fight against you in burning rage
and great fury, with an outstretched hand and a strong
6 arm. I will strike down those who live in this city, men
and cattle alike; they shall die of a great pestilence.
7 After that, says the LORD, I will take Zedekiah king of
Judah, his courtiers and the people, all in this city who
survive pestilence, sword, and famine, and hand them
over to Nebuchadrezzar the king of Babylon, to their
enemies and those who would kill them. He shall put

them to the sword and shall show no pity, no mercy or compassion.

You shall say further to this people, These are the words 8 of the LORD: I offer you now a choice between the way of life and the way of death. Whoever remains in this city 9 shall die by sword, by famine, or by pestilence, but whoever goes out to surrender to the Chaldaeans, who are now besieging you, shall survive; he shall take home his life, and nothing more.[a] I have set my face against this 10 city, meaning to do them harm, not good, says the LORD. It shall be handed over to the king of Babylon, and he shall burn it to the ground.

✷ Several passages in the book, including this one, record consultations of Jeremiah by Zedekiah during the Babylonian siege of Jerusalem in 589–587 B.C. In two of these, 37: 17–21 and 38: 14–28, the prophet is consulted privately by the king himself, whilst in 21: 1–7 and 37: 3–10 the king sends certain state officials to consult him. We may note here that the similarities between 37: 17–21 and 38: 14–28 are such that both accounts are almost certainly based upon the same incident (see the commentary on ch. 38 in vol. 2). There are also similarities between 21: 1–7 and 37: 3–10 but also obvious differences and commentators are divided on the question whether they also are based upon one and the same event. But whether they are or not, the message of the prophet as reported in both is the same: the inevitability of the judgement of God upon his people at the hands of the Babylonians.

The present passage, like the others mentioned above, is composed in the characteristic prose style of the book and contains several typical Deuteronomic expressions (see notes). What precisely Jeremiah said on the occasion described we cannot tell. What can be claimed is that the passage represents

[a] he shall...more: *lit.* his life shall be his booty.

and formulates what was the basis of the prophet's message as a whole, the inevitability of God's judgement upon his people. Why Jeremiah saw judgement to be inevitable is discussed more fully in the commentary on ch. 24 below. Briefly stated, he saw the inner reality of the situation to be that the nation had sunk so deeply into rebellion against God that only a radical break with the past and an entirely new beginning was now possible; only through judgement could renewal come and a new age be brought about by God in which Israel's vocation to be his people would be truly realized. The present passage has nothing to say of the future, but as already noted the complex as a whole turns from judgement to renewal in 23: 1–8. In this way and with specific reference to the monarchy the central theme of the book as a whole – judgement and renewal after judgement (cp. the commentary on 1: 10) – forms the central theme of this individual complex in the book.

Since this passage concerns Zedekiah, it is not immediately obvious why it should have been placed at the head of the complex. From a strictly chronological point of view we would have expected it to have followed the saying concerning Coniah (Jehoiachin) in 22: 24–30. However, as it concerns the judgement announced against not just Zedekiah but also Jerusalem it is possible that the editor placed it here in order to set the judgement announced against the monarchy and individual kings in subsequent oracles and sayings within the framework of the judgement announced against the nation as a whole. Similarly at the end of the complex the future restoration of the monarchy is inseparably bound up with the restoration and renewal of the nation as a whole (23: 1–8).

1. *Pashhur son of Malchiah:* this official, not to be confused with 'Pashhur son of Immer' in 20: 1–6, is later recorded as having belonged to a group of state officials who sought to have Jeremiah executed (38: 1–6). *Zephaniah the priest, son of Maaseiah:* mentioned again in 29: 24–32 as *the priest* who received a letter from Shemaiah the Nehelamite, one of those deported in 597 B.C., complaining about Jeremiah's letter to

the exiles (cp. 29: 1ff.) and demanding suitable action against the prophet.

2. *Nebuchadrezzar:* this is a more correct form of his name than Nebuchadnezzar (in Accadian it is Nabu-kudurri-usur). It is used throughout except in chs. 27–9 where it is 'Nebuchadnezzar' (cp. N.E.B. footnote on 27: 6). Nebuchadrezzar (605–562 B.C.) was the son and successor of Nabopolassar (626–605 B.C.), the first king of the neo-Babylonian empire. Nabopolassar successfully rebelled against the Assyrians and the Assyrian empire was gradually conquered and taken over by him and his even more successful son. Nebuchadrezzar secured his frontiers to the north and north-west by an alliance with the Medes sealed by his marriage to Amyitis, daughter of the king of the Medes. He was succeeded by his son Evil-merodach (Amel Marduk 562–560 B.C.) who is recorded in 2 Kings 25: 27–30 (= Jer. 52: 31–4) as having released Jehoiachin from prison in Babylon. But after two years Evil-merodach was succeeded, probably as the result of a violent *coup d'état*, by his brother-in-law Neriglissar (560–556 B.C.) (possibly to be identified with a Nergalsarezer mentioned in 39: 3). His heir, Labashi-Marduk, reigned only very briefly and was removed from the throne by Nabonidus (556–539 B.C.), the last king of the neo-Babylonian empire who was defeated by Cyrus (550–530 B.C.), the founder and architect of the Persian empire.

Perhaps the LORD will perform a miracle as he has done in past times: the Hebrew reads literally 'perhaps the LORD will deal with us according to all his wonderful acts'. In this context the deliverance of Jerusalem from the Assyrians under Sennacherib during the reign of Hezekiah more than a century before the fall of Jerusalem (cp. 2 Kings 19: 35) springs readily to mind as the sort of *miracle* or 'wonderful act' called for in the present situation.

4. *and I will bring them into the heart of this city:* the meaning of this phrase is obscure. As it stands it can only refer to the *weapons* mentioned immediately before it. Probably we are to understand *weapons* as designating bands of Judaean troops

who were still able at this stage in the siege to operate outside
the city walls and harass the Babylonian encampments. Or was
this phrase originally a marginal gloss, subsequently accident-
ally copied into the text proper, referring to the Babylonians,
that is, that God would bring them into the heart of the city?

5. *in burning rage and great fury:* this phrase also occurs in
32: 37 and elsewhere only in Deut. 29: 28 (there rendered by
N.E.B. as 'in anger, in wrath and great fury'). The phrase
with an outstretched hand and a strong arm occurs also in 32: 21
(cp. 27: 5; 32: 17) and frequently in Deuteronomy and the
Deuteronomic literature (cp. e.g. Deut. 4: 34; 1 Kings 8: 42;
cp. 2 Kings 17: 36).

7. *and shall show no pity, no mercy or compassion:* Nebuchadrezzar was the equal of any ancient Near Eastern potentate
when it came to brutal treatment of his conquered enemies!

8–10. The speech directed against Zedekiah in verses 1–7 is
followed by a short statement again announcing the inevitability of Babylonian victory and setting out the choice which
lay before the inhabitants of Jerusalem. Although this passage,
reporting that the prophet counselled the people to surrender
to the Babylonians, is in prose we have every reason to believe
that Jeremiah did advise such a course of action and because of
this was regarded as a traitor (cp. 38: 17–21). In this, however,
his motives and intentions were misunderstood. That he was
no traitor desiring only the subjugation of his homeland and
countrymen is clear from the fact that when the catastrophe
befell the nation in 587 B.C. he chose to remain in the land and
there work for the future renewal of the nation's life as God's
people (cp. 40: 1–6; 42: 7–22). For Jeremiah the Babylonians
were nothing in themselves but merely the instrument of
judgement in God's hand. As we have seen already, he saw the
inner reality of the situation to be that the nation stood under
inevitable judgement firmly decreed and to be effected by
God; there was simply no escaping this judgement. When he
counselled surrender to the Babylonians, therefore, he was in
effect calling the nation to submission to God's judgement, for

strange as it may at first seem the very act of doing so would itself have been the first step towards future renewal and revival. For this reason it is also incorrect to understand the prophet's message to have been based in any way upon political or military reasoning, as if he had weighed up the 'pros' and 'cons' of the situation in which the nation found itself and then counselled the course of action which seemed to him to be least injurious for the people. It is not impossible that some of those state officials who evidently sympathized with his message (cp. e.g. 26: 24; 36: 25; 38: 7–13) did so because they considered the situation to be so hopeless militarily that they saw the course of action he announced to be the only possible one. But whether or not this is so, Jeremiah was motivated only by his burning conviction that the judgement of God upon the nation was inevitable and the fact that it was to be realized through the success of the Babylonians was merely incidental and most certainly did not arise from any pro-Babylonian sentiment which, in any case, we can be quite certain Jeremiah never had.

8. *the way of life and the way of death:* cp. the similar choice laid before Israel concerning obedience to the terms of the covenant in Deut. 30: 15, 19.

9. *he shall take home his life, and nothing more:* the expression occurs again in 38: 2; 39: 18; 45: 5. As noted in the N.E.B. footnote, the Hebrew is literally 'his life shall be his booty'. Possibly the expression was coined among soldiers. Victorious troops usually acquired booty from their defeated enemies. We can imagine that a soldier, returning *home* from a defeat in which he had a narrow escape, when asked what booty he had, might reply with a mixture of irony and relief: 'my life is my booty!' ✶

THE DUTIES OF THE KING

To the royal house of Judah.   11
   Listen to the word of the LORD:

12   O house of David, these are the words of the LORD:
           Administer justice betimes,
         rescue the victim from his oppressor,
       lest the fire of my fury blaze up and burn unquenched
           because of your evil doings.

※ Ch. 21 continues with a brief poetic oracle stating suc-
cinctly one of the central duties of the monarchy in *Judah*, the
administration of *justice* among the people. The prose passage
at the beginning of the following chapter (22: 1-6) centres on
the same issue. A great many new insights have been gained
by scholars in recent years into the nature of kingship in
ancient Israel. We do not know much about the beliefs
centring on kingship in northern Israel during the monarchic
period there (922-722 B.C.), but a great deal of information
has been adduced from the Old Testament relating to the
office and functions of the Davidic dynasty in Jerusalem. A
Davidic king was no mere figurehead. On the contrary, there
developed in Jerusalem a 'high doctrine' of kingship centring
on the belief that a special covenant existed between Israel's
God Yahweh and the 'house' or dynasty of David as repre-
sented by each succeeding Davidic king (cp. 2 Sam. 7: 11-16;
23: 5). In Ps. 2, a psalm which was probably used at the accession or coronation of a new king, the king is referred to as the
(adopted) son of Yahweh. Thus the king states (verse 7):

           I will repeat the LORD's decree:
         'You are my son,' he said;
             'this day I become your father.'

As God's Messiah ('anointed one') and as his 'son', the person
of the king was sacral, that is, each king stood in a close and
special relation to God (cp. 1 Sam. 26: 11 where *David*,
though in a position to kill Saul, refuses to 'lift a finger against
the LORD's anointed'). Furthermore, the belief was held that
in and through the king prosperity and well-being (Hebrew

shalom) was secured for the nation and safety from its enemies. But the special relationship between the Davidic king and God brought with it solemn obligations, one of the most important of which was the establishment of *justice* and righteousness among the people. Thus Ps. 72, yet another 'royal' psalm, begins with the prayer:

> O God, endow the king with thy own justice,
>   and give thy righteousness to a king's son,
> that he may judge thy people rightly,
>   and deal out justice to the poor and suffering.

The summons to the monarchy in 21: 11–12 is obviously based upon the same belief concerning the duty of a king to *Administer justice* in the nation. Failure to do so would entail judgement (verse 14; cp. Ps. 132: 12). Note that the same belief concerning the solemn obligation of the king to *Administer justice* forms the basis of Isaiah's concept of the future ideal Messiah (Isa. 9: 6–7; 11: 1–4. See also the comments on Jer. 23: 5–6).

AN ORACLE AGAINST JERUSALEM

The LORD says,   13
I am against you who lie in the valley,
    you, the rock in the plain,
you who say, 'Who can come down upon us?
    Who can penetrate our lairs?'
I will punish you as you deserve,   14
    says the LORD,
I will kindle fire on the heathland around you,
and it shall consume everything round about.

✻ Since the *you* referred to in this oracle is the second person singular feminine, commentators are agreed that it is an oracle of judgement against Jerusalem (a city was thought of as the 'mother' of its inhabitants; the villages around it were referred to as its 'daughters'). The context also requires an interpretation of the oracle as concerning Jerusalem. Nevertheless, the descriptions *you who lie in the valley* and *you, the rock in the plain* do not fit Jerusalem. Probably, therefore, we have here a quotation from a poem originally concerning another city, the identity of which we cannot ascertain, which has been inserted here and thus secondarily related to Jerusalem. Probably it was placed after verses 11–12 because of the similar ending of both oracles (note the catchword *fire* in verses 12 and 14). ✻

AGAIN THE DUTIES OF THE KING

22 These were the words of the LORD: Go down to the
2 house of the king of Judah and say this: Listen to the words of the LORD, O king of Judah, you who sit on David's throne, you and your courtiers and your people
3 who come in at these gates. These are the words of the LORD: Deal justly and fairly, rescue the victim from his oppressor, do not ill-treat or do violence to the alien, the orphan or the widow, do not shed innocent blood in this
4 place. If you obey, and only if you obey, kings who sit on David's throne shall yet come riding through these gates in chariots and on horses, with their retinue of courtiers
5 and people. But if you do not listen to my words, then by myself I swear, says the LORD, this house shall become a
6 desolate ruin. For these are the words of the LORD about the royal house of Judah:

> Though you are dear to me as Gilead
>   or as the heights of Lebanon,
> I swear that I will make you a wilderness,
>   a land of unpeopled cities.

I will dedicate an armed host to fight against you,   7
   a ravening horde;
they shall cut your choicest cedars down
   and fling them on the fire.

Men of many nations shall pass by this city and say to   8
one another, 'Why has the LORD done this to such a great
city?' The answer will be, 'Because they forsook their   9
covenant with the LORD their God; they worshipped
other gods and served them.'

＊ Verses 1–5 are in prose and are a Deuteronomic composition.
One has the impression that they are an expansion of the poetic
oracle in 21: 11–12. The attitude of the Deuteronomic authors
to kingship in Israel is ambivalent. On the one hand the law
concerning kingship in Deuteronomy itself (Deut. 17: 14–20)
adopts a critical attitude towards the institution of the monarchy; in seeking to have a king Israel is merely aping 'all the
surrounding nations' (verse 14), whilst some of the narratives
in the Deuteronomic history concerning the origins of the
monarchy in Israel are markedly anti-monarchical in content
(cp. 1 Sam. 8, 12). On the other hand the Deuteronomic
historians, in addition to having some narratives recording the
foundation of the monarchy as resting in the initiative of God
(cp. 1 Sam. 9: 15–10: 16), have placed great emphasis on the
divine promises to David and the existence of a unique
covenant between Israel's God and the Davidic dynasty
(cp. 2 Sam. 7). Similarly the way in which throughout the
books of Kings they have placed the responsibility for the
nation's adherence to the law of God upon the shoulders of
the kings, most of whom are condemned for not having lived
up to this responsibility, reveals a 'high doctrine' of the solemn
obligations of the monarchy in the life of God's people. In
addition, it is possible that the last few verses of 2 Kings
recording the release of Jehoiachin from prison in exile and

his 'rehabilitation' by the Babylonian king Evil-merodach (2 Kings 25: 27–30 = Jer. 52: 31–4) is to be understood as pointing to the conviction that with this event the possibility opened up for a new chapter in the history of the Davidic dynasty. In ending their history with this event the authors may have been hinting at the tenacity of God's promises to David.

Of one thing we can be sure, the Deuteronomic authors throughout their writings demanded of the monarchy strict adherence to God's law (cp. Deut. 17: 18–20) which laid down the statutes and ordinances governing the life of the people of God in the land of Canaan; any king who failed to adhere to it is roundly condemned (cp. the comments on Manasseh in the commentary on Jer. 15: 1–4). In the prose passages in Jeremiah the same conception of the solemn responsibilities of the monarchy is expressed, as here in verses 1–5 but also, as we shall see, in such narratives as chs. 26 and 36. (On hope for the future based upon the promises to David see on 23: 1–6.)

Attached to this prose passage is a short oracle in poetry announcing judgement (verses 6–7). But the object of this judgement is somewhat ambiguous. The N.E.B. translation of the superscription clearly understands the oracle as one of judgement against the Davidic dynasty, 'the royal house of Judah' (verse 6). But the Hebrew is literally 'the house of the king of Judah' and could thus refer to the house in the sense of the palace. Whilst the N.E.B. understanding of the text remains possible, more probably the oracle does refer to the palace. In favour of this is the fact that in the prose passage which precedes it 'the house of the king of Judah' (verse 1) and 'this house' (verse 5) clearly refer to the palace. Furthermore, the nature of the judgement is best understood as referring to a place rather than a dynasty, the destruction of which can scarcely be likened to 'a wilderness' or to 'a land of unpeopled cities' (see further the comments on verse 7 below). In addition the short prose passage which immediately follows this oracle and which centres on the destruction of Jerusalem also renders likely the interpretation of verses 6–7 in terms of the royal palace rather than specifically the royal dynasty. On the form of verses 8–9 see the note on 5: 19. As noted there the same form is found in 9: 12*b*–16 and 16: 10–13.

3. *rescue the victim from his oppressor:* the same phrase occurs in 21: 11 and the word here translated *victim* occurs in the book of Jeremiah only in these two passages. This favours the view, noted above, that 22: 1–5 is an expansion of 21: 11–12.

6. *Gilead:* though noted for the balm associated with it (cp. the note on 8: 22), *Gilead* was also renowned for its forests which are still numerous there today. The fact that *Gilead* is coupled here with *the heights of Lebanon* (see next note) probably indicates that the reference to it here is because of its forests rather than the balm. *the heights of Lebanon:* the forests on the mountains of *Lebanon* were renowned in ancient times for their cedars which are referred to in numerous places in the Old Testament. Cedar wood from *Lebanon* was used extensively by Solomon in building the temple and palace in Jerusalem. In 1 Kings 7: 2–5 part of the palace is named 'the House of the Forest of Lebanon' (cp. also Isa. 22: 8 where it is called 'the House of the Forest').

7. *they shall cut your choicest cedars down:* this is best understood as a reference to the cedar wood, perhaps cedar pillars, employed in the building of the royal palace.

8–9. These two verses are markedly Deuteronomic in form, language and content. They are strikingly similar to the Deuteronomic passage 1 Kings 9: 8–9. ✲

CONCERNING SHALLUM

Weep not for the dead nor brood over his loss.   10
    Weep rather for him who has gone away,
    for he shall never return,
    never again see the land of his birth.

11 For these are the words of the LORD concerning Shallum
   son of Josiah, king of Judah, who succeeded his father on
12 the throne and has gone away: He shall never return; he
   shall die in the place of his exile and never see this land
   again.

* The remainder of ch. 22 comprises a number of sayings in
both prose and poetry concerning the last three kings of Judah
before the fateful reign of Zedekiah. The first is a short poetic
oracle followed by a brief prose passage which interprets it
and makes it clear the object of the lament in the poetic oracle
is Shallum (Jehoahaz). This king succeeded his father Josiah
after the latter had been tragically killed in fighting against the
Egyptian Pharaoh Necho at Megiddo in 609 B.C. In 2 Kings
23: 30-5 it is recorded that after his father's death he was
acclaimed king, but that Pharaoh Necho, following up his
victory at Megiddo and evidently distrusting the new king,
deposed him and had Jehoiakim made king instead. Jehoahaz
was exiled to Egypt and died there. He had reigned as king of
Judah for but a few months in 609 B.C.

10. *Weep not for the dead:* a reference to Josiah: his fate is
regarded as better than that of his exiled son.

11. *Shallum son of Josiah:* this appears to have been the king's
personal name. His regnal or throne name was Jehoahaz.
There is evidence that Judaean kings on accession to the throne
adopted a new name, that is, a regnal or throne name. For
example, Solomon was probably this king's regnal name; he
was called Jedidiah before his accession (cp. 2 Sam. 12: 25).
Similarly, before his enthronement Zedekiah was called
Mattaniah (cp. 2 Kings 24: 17). *

CONCERNING JEHOIAKIM

13 Shame on the man who builds his house by unjust means
   and completes its roof-chambers by fraud,

    making his countrymen work without payment,
    giving them no wage for their labour!
Shame on the man who says, 'I will build a spacious   14
    house
    with airy roof-chambers,
set windows in it, panel it with cedar
    and paint it with vermilion'!
    If your cedar is more splendid,   15
    does that prove you a king?
Think of your father: he ate and drank,
dealt justly and fairly; all went well with him.
    He dispensed justice to the lowly and poor;[a]   16
did not this show he knew me? says the LORD.
But you have no eyes, no thought for anything but gain,   17
    set only on the innocent blood you can shed,
    on cruel acts of tyranny.

Therefore these are the words of the LORD concerning   18
Jehoiakim son of Josiah, king of Judah:

For him no mourner shall say, 'Alas, brother, dear
    brother!'
no one say, 'Alas, lord and master!'
    He shall be buried like a dead ass,   19
    dragged along and flung out
    beyond the gates of Jerusalem.

✶ These verses comprise two oracles, the first condemning the injustice, avarice and tyranny of Jehoiakim, the second announcing a terrible judgement upon him. Of the various individual kings condemned by Jeremiah none was more bitterly attacked by him than Jehoiakim.

   [a] *Prob. rdg.; Heb. adds* all went well (*repeated from verse 15*).

13. *his countrymen:* the word here translated is literally 'his neighbour': the freedom and rights of one's neighbour in Israel were as much to be observed and guarded by the king as by his subjects. In Israel the king and his carpenter were 'neighbours'. We may recall that one of the major grievances the Israelites had against Solomon was his tyrannical enslavement of many in his building operations in Jerusalem and elsewhere (cp. 1 Kings 5: 13f.; 12: 3f.).

15. *If your cedar is more splendid:* the Hebrew is literally 'though you compete in cedar'. It seems that Jehoiakim was vain enough to imagine that the splendour and magnificence of his palace would enhance his stature as *king*.

he ate and drank: he is unfavourably compared with his revered *father* Josiah who lived *well* and contentedly (that is the force of the expression *he ate and drank* in this context) and yet attended to his royal duties and the solemn responsibilities required of a *king* by God. One of the main motifs in ch. 36 is also the contrast between Jehoiakim and Josiah.

19. *He shall be buried like a dead ass:* the bitterness of the judgement here announced against Jehoiakim is heightened by this, for the *ass* as an animal which neither parted the hoof nor chewed the cud was regarded in Israel's dietary laws as unclean (cp. Lev. 11: 1–8; Deut. 14: 3–8). We have no evidence that Jehoiakim died anything other than a peaceful death or received anything other than a normal burial. There is no evidence for the view, advanced by some commentators, that his body was later disinterred and dishonoured. ✳

ALAS FOR JERUSALEM!

20   Get up into Lebanon and cry aloud,
          make your voice heard in Bashan,
      cry aloud from Abarim, for all who befriend you are
          broken.

I spoke to you in your days of prosperous ease,   21
　　but you said, 'I will not listen.'
This is how you behaved since your youth;
　　never have you obeyed me.
The wind shall carry away all your friends,[a]   22
your lovers shall depart into exile.
Then you will be put to shame and abashed
　　for all your evil deeds.[b]
You dwellers in Lebanon, who make your nests   23
　　among the cedars,
　　how you will groan when the pains come upon you,
　　like the pangs of a woman in labour!

✶ The position of this address to Jerusalem (in the Hebrew
the second person singular feminine form of address is used,
Jerusalem being personified as a woman; cp. the comments
on 21: 13-14) between the oracles concerning Jehoiakim and
those concerning Jehoiachin which follow in verses 24-30
suggests that it was composed in 597 B.C. shortly before the
capitulation of Jerusalem to Nebuchadrezzar and the first
deportation of Judaeans, including Jehoiachin, to Babylon in
that same year.

20. Jerusalem is summoned to bewail her fate far and wide,
in *Lebanon* in the north, in *Bashan* in the north-east in Trans-
jordan, and in *Abarim* in Moab in the south-east. *Abarim* is a
mountainous region in northern Moab overlooking the Dead
Sea and the Jordan Valley. Num. 33: 47-8 records that the
Israelites encamped there on the eve of their entry into the
land of Canaan. Nebo was the principal peak in this region and
it was from Nebo that Moses is said to have looked across to
the promised land and at Nebo that he is believed to have died
(cp. Num. 27: 12; Deut. 32: 49).

22. *your friends* and *your lovers* here could be a reference to

[a] *Or* shepherds.   [b] *Or* calamities.

Judah's allies (cp. also Hos. 8: 9 where Assyria as Israel's ally is referred to as her 'lovers') or, if the reading 'shepherds' (cp. N.E.B. footnote) is preferred, to the leaders and nobility of Jerusalem deported in 597 B.C. (cp. 2 Kings 24: 12ff.).

23. *You dwellers in Lebanon: Lebanon* is here used figuratively for Jerusalem itself (cp. verse 6 above) and not, as in verse 20, for the land of *Lebanon*. ✶

CONCERNING JEHOIACHIN

24 By my life, says the LORD, Coniah son of Jehoiakim, king of Judah, shall be the signet-ring on my right hand
25 no longer. Yes, Coniah, I will pull you off. I will hand you over to those who seek your life, to those you fear, to Nebuchadrezzar king of Babylon and to the Chaldaeans.
26 I will fling you headlong, you and the mother who gave you birth, into another land, a land where you were not
27 born; and there shall you both die. They shall never come back to their own land, the land for which they long.

28   This man, Coniah, then, is he a mere puppet, contemptible and broken, only a thing unwanted? Why else are he and his children flung out headlong and hurled into a country they do not know?

29,30   O land, land, land, hear the words of the LORD: These are the words of the LORD: Write this man down as stripped of all honour, one who in his own life shall not prosper, nor shall he leave descendants to sit in prosperity on David's throne or rule again in Judah.

✶ Jehoiachin, here referred to as Coniah, was the son and successor of Jehoiakim. The latter, having rebelled against Babylon in 601 B.C., died before the Babylonian move to quash his rebellion was completed. Jehoiachin succeeded him

but reigned for only three months before Nebuchadrezzar
conquered Jerusalem in 597 B.C. The young king (he was eighteen years old) was taken together with his household and
many others from Judah into exile in Babylon where he
eventually died (cp. Jer. 52: 31–4 = 2 Kings 25: 27–30). The
Babylonians put his uncle Mattaniah, whose name as king was
Zedekiah, on the throne of Judah. Zedekiah was the last king
of Judah before the final destruction of the state in 587 B.C.
Early in the period after the exile Jehoiachin's grandson
Zerubbabel, who became governor of Judah under the Per-
sians, was the centre of renewed hopes for a restoration of the
monarchy in Judah (cp. Hag. 2: 20–3). It is possible that the
release of Jehoiachin from prison in exile by Evil-merodach
in 562 B.C. (cp. the commentary on 52: 31–4 in vol. 2) already
gave rise to such hopes. But nothing came of them and we
do not know what became of Zerubbabel. The present passage
knows nothing of these hopes; what is here stated accords
with historical fact: neither Jehoiachin nor any of his sons
returned to the throne of Judah.

24. *Coniah:* this was probably his personal or private name,
Jehoiachin being his throne-name. *the signet-ring:* such rings,
used for impressing the owner's signature into a wax seal on a
document, were normally made of gold and often set with
precious stones. The figure of the *signet-ring*, valuable and
precious to its owner, was also applied to Jehoiachin's grandson Zerubbabel (cp. Hag. 2: 23).

26. *you and the mother who gave you birth:* cp. 13: 18 and 2
Kings 24: 11f.

30. *stripped of all honour:* the word here translated can also
mean 'childless' and is rendered in this way in several English
translations. But Jehoiachin was not childless (cp. 1 Chron.
3: 17) and the N.E.B. rendering makes better sense. ✲

PROMISES FOR THE FUTURE

23 Shame on the shepherds who let the sheep of my flock
2 scatter and be lost! says the LORD. Therefore these are the
words of the LORD the God of Israel about the shepherds
who tend my people: You have scattered and dispersed
my flock. You have not watched over them; but I am
watching you to punish you for your evil doings, says the
3 LORD. I will myself gather the remnant of my sheep from
all the lands to which I have dispersed them. I will bring
them back to their homes, and they shall be fruitful and
4 increase. I will appoint shepherds to tend them; they shall
never again know fear or dismay or punishment. This is
the very word of the LORD.

5   The days are now coming, says the LORD,
       when I will make a righteous Branch spring from
           David's line,
       a king who shall rule wisely,
       maintaining law and justice in the land.
6   In his days Judah shall be kept safe,
       and Israel[a] shall live undisturbed.
       This is the name to be given to him:
           The LORD is our Righteousness.

7   Therefore the days are coming, says the LORD, when
men shall no longer swear, 'By the life of the LORD who
8 brought Israel up from Egypt', but, 'By the life of the
LORD who brought the descendants of the Israelites back
from a northern land and from all the lands to which he[b]
had dispersed them, to live again on their own soil.'

[a] *Or, with one form of Sept.,* Jerusalem.   [b] *So Sept., cp. 16: 15; Heb.* I.

✻ The message of judgement in chs. 21–2 now turns to one of promises of future restoration for both the nation and the dynasty. This passage comprises three separate sayings. The first (verses 1–4) continues the condemnation of, and judgement upon, the monarchy, the 'shepherds' who have corrupted God's 'flock' Israel, leading and encouraging the nation's apostasy. At the same time it announces the future restoration of the nation from exile and the appointment by God of 'shepherds' who would, unlike their predecessors, care for and tend the nation. This saying, which is composed in prose, appears to presuppose the exile and probably comes from a Deuteronomic author. It is followed by a saying in poetry (verses 5–6; cp. 33: 15–16) promising the coming of an ideal king, 'a righteous Branch' of David's dynasty who will rule the nation wisely. Finally, appended to these sayings is a short saying in prose (verses 7–8) promising deliverance of the nation from exile in a new exodus which would surpass the ancient exodus of Israel from bondage in Egypt. This saying also presupposes the exile and is probably from the Deuteronomic authors, who developed Jeremiah's preaching in the period of the exile, rather than from the prophet himself.

1. *Shame on the shepherds:* the word here translated *Shame* is better rendered 'Woe!'. The saying is one of judgement upon the rulers of the nation rather than one of mere condemnation and rebuke as the rendering *Shame* tends to suggest.

3. *I will myself gather the remnant of my sheep:* the future restoration of the *remnant* of the nation from exile in Babylon is one of the main themes of the book of Jeremiah. Chapters such as 24 and 40–4 make it clear that the *remnant* of the nation with whom and through whom the future of God's people would be brought about were those who had been exiled to Babylon rather than those who had remained in the homeland or the group of exiles who fled to Egypt after the assassination of Gedaliah (cp. 24: 8).

5. *I will make a righteous Branch spring from David's line:* the same promise using a similar metaphor is found in Isa. 11: 1.

The term *Branch* later appears as a Messianic title in Zech. 3: 8; 6: 12. *a king who shall rule wisely, maintaining law and justice in the land:* in this coming *king* the true and proper functions of kingship would be realized (see the commentary on 21: 11–12).

6. *The LORD is our Righteousness:* many commentators see in this a direct allusion to King Zedekiah, Jeremiah's contemporary, whose name means 'Yahweh is my righteousness', and understand it to have been a biting comment on that king by the prophet who here announces the coming of a king who would, unlike Zedekiah, establish and foster righteousness in the nation. But though this could have been the intention of the oracle, it must be remembered that the terminology of *Righteousness* was firmly anchored in the 'ideology' of kingship in ancient Israel so that the use of this terminology here need not imply any allusion to Zedekiah. Furthermore, 'messianism' does not appear to have played much part in Jeremiah's preaching; elsewhere in the book only 30: 8f. and 33: 17 are concerned with the coming of an ideal king and both of these passages are themselves probably not from Jeremiah. For this reason it is possible that the saying here in verses 5–6 comes from a later period than that of Jeremiah.

7–8. See the comments on 16: 14–15. This saying is more appropriate here than in ch. 16. It presupposes the exile and this together with its style indicate the probability that it was composed by a Deuteronomic author. ✶

(B) DENUNCIATIONS OF FALSE PROPHECY

✶ The passage 23: 9–40 comprises a number of originally separate sayings centring on the problem of false prophecy. The first three (verses 9–12, 13–15, 16–22) are composed in poetry and come from Jeremiah. The remaining two passages (verses 23–32, 33–40) are composed for the most part in prose and come from a Deuteronomic author. They evidence the continued concern with the problem of false prophecy in the period after the time of Jeremiah. ✶

A LAND FULL OF ADULTERERS

On the prophets.   9
    Deep within me my heart is broken,
    there is no strength in my bones;
    because of the LORD, because of his dread words
    I have become like a drunken man,
    like a man overcome with wine.
    For the land is full of adulterers,   10
    and because of them the earth lies parched,
      the wild pastures have dried up.
    The course that they run is evil,
      and their powers are misused.
    For prophet and priest alike are godless;   11
I have come upon the evil they are doing even in my
      own house.
      This is the very word of the LORD.

Therefore the path shall turn slippery beneath their   12
      feet;
they shall be dispersed in the dark and shall fall there.
For I will bring disaster on them when their day of
      reckoning comes.
      This is the very word of the LORD.

✻ Once again Jeremiah describes the nation's apostasy in
terms of 'adultery' and again it is a reference to the widespread practice of the Canaanite cult of Baal with its sordid
fertility rites. The leaders of such apostasy are the prophets and
priests. Their day of reckoning is imminent.

   10. *and because of them the earth lies parched:* far from producing
the desired fertility of the land which the cult they engaged in
was supposed to create, their 'adultery' has had the opposite

effect: the land lies *parched* and barren, for they do not acknowledge that it is Yahweh and not Baal who is the source of the
good of the land.

11. *I have come upon the evil they are doing even in my own
house:* the temple itself had become the scene of pagan cults
innovated and encouraged by the cultic personnel there, the
priests and prophets. The reformation carried out by Josiah
in 621 B.C. sought to get rid of foreign cults from the temple
and its precincts (cp. 2 Kings 23) and no doubt succeeded for
a while. But after his death (609 B.C.) the rot set in again and the
preaching of Jeremiah and Ezekiel leaves us in no doubt that
pagan cults thrived in Jerusalem again during the last years of
the state of Judah. ✶

THE PROPHETS AS LEADERS OF THE
NATION'S SINFULNESS

13   I found the prophets of Samaria men of no sense:
          they prophesied in Baal's name and led my people
               Israel astray.

14   In the prophets of Jerusalem I see a thing most horrible:
          adulterers and hypocrites that they are,
               they encourage evildoers,
          so that no man turns back from his sin;
        to me all her inhabitants are like Sodom and
               Gomorrah.

15   These then are the words of the LORD of Hosts concern-
      ing the prophets:

        I will give them wormwood to eat
          and a bitter poison to drink;
             for a godless spirit has spread over all the land
             from the prophets of Jerusalem.

✲ 14. *adulterers:* the context requires that we understand the adultery here referred to in the literal sense of the word and not as a metaphor for cultic apostasy as in several other passages. This seems clear from the ensuing statement that these *prophets* encouraged the people in their sinfulness. It is further indicated by the comparison of the people with the *inhabitants* of *Sodom and Gomorrah*, the supremely sinful cities. *hypocrites:* the Hebrew is literally 'who walk in the lie *or* falsehood'. Elsewhere these *prophets* are denounced as having taught and preached false-hood. Here their way of life, which exemplifies what they preach, is condemned. Thus by their preaching as well as their way of life they foster and *encourage* sinfulness in the nation.

15. *I will give them wormwood to eat and a bitter poison to drink:* see the comment on 9: 15. *for a godless spirit has spread over all the land from the prophets of Jerusalem: godless spirit* translates a word meaning 'profanity', 'pollution'. These *prophets* are condemned for having fostered and encouraged the nation's apostasy and sinfulness. Neither by their own example nor by their teaching did they lead the people in loyalty to God and obedience to his moral commands. ✲

I DID NOT SEND THESE PROPHETS

These are the words of the LORD of Hosts:

> Do not listen to what the prophets say,   16
>   who buoy you up with false hopes;
> the vision they report springs from their own
>   imagination,
>   it is not from the mouth of the LORD.
> They say to those who spurn the word of the LORD,   17
>   'Prosperity shall be yours';
> and to all who follow the promptings of their own
>   stubborn heart they say,
>   'No disaster shall befall you.'

18   But which of them has stood in the council of the
          LORD,
      seen him and heard his word?
      Which of them has listened to his word and
          obeyed?

19   See what a scorching wind has gone out from the
          LORD,
      a furious whirlwind;
      it whirls round the heads of the wicked.

20   The LORD's anger is not to be turned aside,
      until he has accomplished and fulfilled his deep
          designs.
      In days to come you will fully understand.

21   I did not send these prophets, yet they went in haste;
      I did not speak to them, yet they prophesied.

22   If they have stood in my council,
      let them proclaim my words to my people
      and turn them from their evil course and their evil
          doings.

✻ The prophets here referred to were condemned by
Jeremiah for beguiling the nation into a false sense of security.
The message of prosperity they proclaimed rested upon a
totally mistaken conception of the relationship between God
and his people, indeed upon a base conception of the very
nature of God. They no doubt pointed to God's election of
Israel to be his people, to his choice of Zion to be his holy and
therefore inviolable dwelling-place, as well as to his promises to
David and his descendants upon the throne of Judah. All this,
they proclaimed, guaranteed the security of the people among
the nations round about. But what they failed to acknowledge
and preach was that God's goodness towards his people, his
election of them, demanded a response from them in terms of

radical obedience to his righteous will. Their 'doctrine' of God was thus devoid of any awareness of his holiness and the demand for holiness from those called to be his people. Jeremiah saw the reality of the situation to be that the nation by its sinfulness had forfeited its divine election; everything about its life was a denial of its calling to be God's people. Consequently, judgement was the message for the time and any prophet who preached otherwise betrayed himself as one who did not stand 'in the council of the LORD'.

16. *the vision they report springs from their own imagination:* these prophets did not 'wait upon the LORD'. Their own conception of God and his relationship to the nation was the sole source of their preaching.

17. *to all who follow the promptings of their own stubborn heart they say, 'No disaster shall befall you':* these prophets saw only God's commitment to the nation and indeed understood it as obliging God to sustain and defend its life come what may. But they were blind to the solemn demand for righteousness and holiness which Israel's calling laid upon it. Hence they failed to convict the nation of its sinfulness.

18. *But which of them has stood in the council of the LORD: the council of the LORD* was conceived of as the heavenly court over which God presided and where his righteous purposes were declared. The true prophet was believed to be one who by his calling and communion with God was privy to the purposes of God made known in the heavenly *council.*

19–20. These verses are also in 30:23–4 where, they have been supplemented by the addition of 31:1. In ch. 23 they would seem to interrupt the connection between verse 18 and verses 21–2. But they are to be seen as emphasizing the true nature of what God had declared at this time against the message of prosperity and well-being announced by the false prophets. For this reason their originality here need not be questioned.

20. *In days to come you will fully understand:* one has only to bear in mind the hostility towards Jeremiah and his message by his countrymen to realize how incomprehensible and

unacceptable they found his preaching. The judgement he announced ran counter to all they had been taught and believed about God's commitment to them as his elect people. *In days to come* a greater and nobler vision of God and his purposes would open their eyes to the truth of what was now being proclaimed to them. They would learn that only through the judgement now to befall them could they be drawn into a new and deeper relationship with God and realize as never before what their vocation to be his people meant and entailed for them and the world. The shallowness of the preaching of the false prophets would then be manifest.

22. *and turn them from their evil course and their evil doings:* one of the marks of the true prophet was that he saw a direct and inner relationship between the nation's election by God and the necessity of its response to him in terms of holiness and righteousness. One of his primary tasks was therefore continually to convict the people of their sinfulness. ✲

WHAT HAS CHAFF TO DO WITH GRAIN?

23 Am I a god only near at hand,*a* not far away?*b*
24 Can a man hide in any secret place and I not see him?*a*
    Do I not fill heaven and earth?
        This is the very word of the LORD.

25 I have heard what the prophets say, the prophets who
    speak lies in my name and cry, 'I have had a dream, a
26 dream!' How long will it be till they change their tune,
    these prophets who prophesy lies and give voice to their
27 own inventions? By these dreams which they tell one
    another these men think they will make my people forget
    my name, as their fathers forgot my name for the name of*c*

[a] So Sept; Heb. adds says the LORD.
[b] Am I...away?: or, with Sept., I am a god near at hand, and not far away.   [c] for the name of: or by their worship of.

Baal. If a prophet has a dream, let him tell his dream; if he 28
has my word, let him speak my word in truth. What has
chaff to do with grain? says the LORD. Do not my words 29
scorch[a] like fire? says the LORD. Are they not like a
hammer that splinters rock? I am against the prophets, 30
says the LORD, who steal my words from one another for
their own use. I am against the prophets, says the LORD, 31
who concoct words of their own and then say, 'This is his
very word.' I am against the prophets, says the LORD, who 32
dream lies and retail them, misleading my people with
wild and reckless falsehoods. It was not I who sent them
or commissioned them, and they will do this people no
good. This is the very word of the LORD.

* Apart from verses 23–4 this passage is composed in prose
and though presupposing, if not based upon, a saying of
Jeremiah condemning false prophecy it owes its present form
to those who preserved and further developed his message in
the period after his ministry, that is, the period of the exile.
This passage is evidence of the ongoing concern with false
prophecy in the years after 587 B.C. The tragic events of that
year had shown the prophets who had announced prosperity
to the nation to have been bogus. The condemnation of them
by Jeremiah had been vindicated. The author of Lamentations,
writing in the period after the destruction of Jerusalem,
bewailed the way in which these prophets had misled the
nation (Lam. 2: 14); Ezekiel at the same time bitterly attacked
and condemned these same false prophets (Ezek. 13). So also
those who preserved Jeremiah's words further emphasized the
evil done by such prophets and thereby reinforced his condemnation of them and put the people on guard against being
further beguiled and misled by them during the period of the
exile (cp. 29: 15–23). The condemnation of false prophecy

[a] scorch: *prob. rdg.; Heb.* thus.

and the disillusionment with prophecy which must have arisen in the period of the exile contributed, probably to no small extent, to the eventual disappearance of prophecy in the period after the exile.

23-4. These verses express what we today would refer to as the transcendence and immanence of God. God is exalted above all yet is also active in the affairs of men and knows the secrets of the human heart. Nothing is hidden from his all-seeing eye. Though false prophets may deceive men, their doings are known by God for what they are. Such a statement forms an apt preface to what follows, even though it did not originally belong with it.

27. By their impressive-sounding *dreams* which they related to the people these prophets beguiled them into a false sense of security so that they remained unaware of God's demands upon their lives and his divine purposes for the nation. Though they claimed to speak in the *name* of Yahweh they were no better than their predecessors who had fostered and led the nation's apostasy to the worship of *Baal*.

28. *If a prophet has a dream, let him tell his dream: if he has my word, let him speak my word in truth:* the point of this statement is indicated by what follows: *What has chaff to do with grain?* The dreams of these prophets are no more the word of God than the *chaff* is to be thought of as the *grain*.

29. *Do not my words scorch like fire? says the LORD. Are they not like a hammer that splinters rock?:* the word of God was such that it cut deep into the minds of those who received and proclaimed it and those who heard it, challenging them, convicting and exhorting them and demanding a response of radical obedience. As such it was of a totally different quality from the complacent message spoken by the false prophets whose 'easy' words served only to blind men to the radical demand on their loyalty and devotion by the true word of God.

30. *who steal my words from one another for their own use:* so devoid of inspiration and so bogus were they in their pre-

tensions to be prophets that these men had to resort to plagiar-
izing the *words* of other prophets and prolcaim them as their
own!

31. *who concoct words of their own:* where they are unable to
plagiarize, they *concoct* some impressive-sounding saying
calculated to convince the people of its divine source. *

THE BURDEN OF THE LORD

When you are asked by this people or by a prophet or 33
priest what the burden of the LORD's message is, you shall
answer, You are his burden, and I shall throw you down,
says the LORD. If prophet or priest or layman uses the term 34
'the LORD's burden', I will punish that man and his family.
The form of words you shall use in speaking amongst 35
yourselves is: 'What answer has the LORD given?' or,
'What has the LORD said?' You shall never again mention 36
'the burden of the LORD'; that is reserved for the man to
whom he entrusts his message. If you do, you will make
nonsense of the words of the living God, the LORD of
Hosts our God. This is the form you shall use in speaking 37
to a prophet: 'What answer has the LORD given?' or,
'What has the LORD said?' But to any of you who do say, 38
'the burden of the LORD', the LORD speaks thus: Because
you say, 'the burden of the LORD', though I sent to tell
you not to say it, therefore I myself will carry you like a 39
burden[a] and throw you down, casting out of my sight
both you and the city which I gave to you and to your
forefathers. I will inflict on you endless reproach, endless 40
shame which shall never be forgotten.

[a] carry you like a burden: *so some MSS.; others* forget you.

✻ The substance of this passage is that the prophetic office is henceforth to be taken with utmost seriousness. Impostors will incur God's judgement; only those to whom he entrusts his message are to proclaim it.

33. *You are his burden:* this is a play upon the word *burden*. Within the context of prophecy the 'burden of the LORD' was 'the word of the LORD'. Perhaps the usage of this word *burden* was prompted by the experience that the word *of the LORD* was by its demanding and challenging nature a *burden* placed upon both the *prophet* who received it and those to whom it was proclaimed. Here the *burden of the LORD* is said to be the people who are, as we might paraphrase it, a 'burden *upon* the LORD' which he will cast down.

36. *If you do, you will make nonsense of the words of the living God:* the evident proliferation of people claiming to be prophets had brought the prophetic office into disrepute. Henceforth anyone claiming to speak *the burden of the LORD* who had not been called to do so would suffer the judgement of God. ✻

Two visions

24 THIS IS WHAT THE LORD SHOWED ME: I saw two baskets of figs set out[a] in front of the sanctuary of the LORD. This was after Nebuchadrezzar king of Babylon had deported from Jerusalem Jeconiah son of Jehoiakim, king of Judah, with the officers of Judah, the craftsmen 2 and the smiths,[b] and taken them to Babylon. In one basket the figs were very good, like the figs that are first ripe; in the other the figs were very bad, so bad that they were not 3 fit to eat. The LORD said to me, 'What are you looking at,

[a] set out: *prob. rdg., cp. Sept.;* Heb. appointed.
[b] the smiths: *or* the harem.

Jeremiah?' 'Figs,' I answered, 'the good very good, and
the bad so bad that they are not fit to eat.' Then this word 4
came to me from the LORD: These are the words of the 5
LORD the God of Israel: I count the exiles of Judah whom
I sent away from this place to the land of the Chaldaeans
as good as these good figs. I will look upon them meaning 6
to do them good, and I will restore them to their land; I
will build them up and not pull them down, plant them
and not uproot them. I will give them the wit to know me, 7
for I am the LORD; they shall become my people and I will
become their God, for they will come back to me with all
their heart. But Zedekiah king of Judah, his officers and 8
the survivors of Jerusalem, whether they remain in this
land or live in Egypt – all these I will treat as bad figs, says
the LORD, so bad that they are not fit to eat. I will make 9
them repugnant*a* to all the kingdoms of the earth, a
reproach, a by-word, an object-lesson and a thing of
ridicule wherever I drive them. I will send against them 10
sword, famine, and pestilence until they have vanished
from the land which I gave to them and to their forefathers.

* The historical background of this vision of Jeremiah
prompted by the two baskets of figs is clear (cp. verse 1). It
appears that after the deportation of Jehoiachin and other
leading Judaeans in 597 B.C. (cp. 2 Kings 24: 10–17) a new air
of optimism arose in Judah. The conviction grew that all was
now well for the future. We know from ch. 27 that Zedekiah
soon became involved in a conspiracy for further rebellion
against the Babylonians, whilst from ch. 28 we gather that it
was widely believed that those who had been exiled in 597 B.C.

[*a*] *So Sept.; Heb. adds* a disaster.

were shortly to be brought back home. Jeremiah unrelentingly declared that the hopes which thus arose were false. That God would bring about a new beginning for his people in the future was assured, but that new beginning would be effected through those who had been exiled. Meanwhile Judah itself was yet to face a judgement more rigorous and far-reaching than had yet befallen it.

When we ask why Jeremiah countered the optimism of his fellow-countrymen with such a dismal message, the answer lies in his own deeper understanding of God's purposes for the future of his people and the full realization of their election and vocation to be such. Like his prophetic predecessors such as Hosea, Amos and Isaiah he perceived the inner reality of the situation to be that Israel had sunk so deeply into sin and apostasy that she had forfeited her divine election. At the same time and notwithstanding Israel's rebellion, God's purposes in electing her remained firm. Israel was now helpless and faced inevitable judgement. Yet God through that judgement would create a new beginning for his people; judgement would be followed by new birth and revival. Jeremiah's contemporary Ezekiel saw the new beginning to be like the resurrection of dead bones (Ezek. 37: 1–14), whilst the anonymous prophet of the exile, whose oracles are contained in Isa. 40–55 (usually referred to as Deutero-Isaiah), announced to the exiles in Babylon that God was about to lead them forth in a new exodus which would far surpass in glory the original exodus from Egypt and bring them back triumphantly to their homeland (Isa. 43 : 16–20; 48 : 20f.; 51 : 9–11). But for both Ezekiel and Deutero-Isaiah that new beginning was made possible only through judgement, for only in that way could the nation's rebellious past be blotted out and a new and totally different future for her as God's people be brought about. Thus Deutero-Isaiah's prophecies began with the declaration that Israel had now 'fulfilled her term of bondage' and had 'received at the LORD's hand double measure for all her sins' (Isa. 40: 2).

So also was it with Jeremiah, as ch. 24 and similar passages throughout the book make clear. He saw the hollowness of the hopes held by the people after 597 B.C. and how they failed to see that nothing less than a total break with their sinful past was now the only way in which the future of Israel as God's people was possible. Hence his message that their bondage to Babylon was inevitable and the very will of God and his declaration that further rebellion against Babylon was rebellion against God himself (cp. e.g. ch. 27). This explains also why the exiles are regarded in ch. 24 as elsewhere in the book as those who were now the object of God's promises of blessing and restoration for the future. For the judgement of the exile more than anything else was seen by the great prophets of the time as the very means whereby the new beginning for God's people was to be achieved. Hence it is not surprising that the three major collections of prophecies from the period of the exile regard the exiles in Babylon as the object of God's re-newed activity to save and renew his people.

Furthermore, this is also true of the Deuteronomic theology (cp. Deut. 30: 1–10). Hence it is not surprising that many of the prose passages in Jeremiah, centring on the theme of Israel's future after judgement, assumed the form in which we now have them at the hands of Deuteronomic authors and editors. As we shall see, this is the case with ch. 29 and with the historical narrative in 40: 7 – 44: 30. But it is the case too with ch. 24 which is also written in the characteristic prose style of the book. Indeed this chapter offers an excellent example of how a saying originally spoken by Jeremiah was subsequently taken up by Deuteronomic editors and further developed by them in order to press home a message upon the minds of the generation to whom they addressed themselves, and at the same time provides the key to the understanding of other prose passages in the book (see the commentary on 29: 16–20 and 40: 7 – 44: 30 in vol. 2).

The reason Jeremiah's original saying in this instance was further developed is obvious, for in drawing a sharp distinction between those who had undergone judgement and were in exile after 597 B.C. and those who had been untouched by that judgement and remained in Judah, it would have continued to be a source of hope for those in exile throughout the period of the exile. Not only those who had been deported in 597 B.C. but also those exiled after 587 B.C. would have seen in it the declaration of their future renewal and restoration. Furthermore, not only would they have seen this vision as announcing their salvation: they would also have understood it as a rejection of any belief that the new beginning planned for his people by God would be brought about amongst those who had remained in Judah during the period of the exile. Indeed it is in this connection that we find the clearest evidence that this passage assumed its present form in the exilic period proper, that is, after 587 B.C. For verse 8 announces judgement against those who fled to Egypt and this almost certainly presupposes the murder of Gedaliah and the subsequent flight to Egypt of the 'remnant' left in Judah after 587 B.C. (43: 1–7). (We shall see that the history of this 'remnant' forms the main theme of the historical narrative contained in 40: 6 – 44: 30.) Thus, to sum up, Jeremiah's vision as developed by the Deuteronomic editor during the period of the exile had a theological and a polemical purpose: it proclaimed the exiles in Babylon to be the true remnant of Israel through whom alone renewal and restoration would be wrought by God, as against those who either remained in Judah or lived in Egypt during the period of the exile.

3. *What are you looking at, Jeremiah?:* the manner in which this vision came to *Jeremiah* may be compared with that of the almond in early bloom in 1: 11–12 and the boiling cauldron in 1: 13–14 as also with the vision prompted by the spoilt vessel in the potter's workshop in 18: 3–4. We may also compare it with the visions of Amos reported in Amos 7: 1–9 and 8: 1–3.

6. *I will build them up and not pull them down, plant them and not uproot them:* we have already come across this terminology

(e.g. 1: 10; 12: 14–17) and it will appear again (e.g. 37: 27–8), and we have seen that it centres on one of the main themes of the book as a whole, the theme of judgement and renewal after judgement.

7. *I will give them the wit to know me:* literally 'I will give them a heart to know me'. This promise is clearly closely similar to the promise in 31: 33 and 32: 38f. with all of which we may compare Deut. 30: 6 where God announces to the exiles that he will 'circumcise' their hearts. The promise given here takes us right to the heart of the problem of Israel's future as God's people. Through the centuries Israel had shown herself unwilling to obey God's righteous law. What eventually became clear, however, was that Israel had not merely been unwilling to obey; she was unable to do so. The problem of her future was, therefore, how this inherent inability to be faithful could be overcome. That is, how could it be ensured that the same sinful 'heart' would not again assert itself and again carry the nation into rebellion against God as it had persistently done in the past? The only possible answer to this was that God by sheer miracle would so transform the *heart* of his *people* that they would henceforth both perceive and be able to perform his righteous will. The same promise is given in Ezek. 36: 26: 'I will give you a new heart and put a new spirit within you; I will take the heart of stone from your body and give you a heart of flesh. I will put my spirit into you and make you conform to my statutes, keep my laws and live by them.'

8. *whether they remain in this land or live in Egypt:* the Hebrew text reads literally 'and those who are living in the land of Egypt'. As we have seen, this almost certainly has in mind those who, after the murder of Gedaliah, fled to *Egypt* against the command of God announced to them by Jeremiah (42: 7 – 43: 7). As such it indicates strongly, as we have seen, that the passage in its present form was composed after 587 B.C. and that those who composed it sought to bring up to date, so to speak, one of Jeremiah's prophecies. ✻

A CONCLUDING SUMMARY

25 This came to Jeremiah as the word concerning all the people of Judah in the fourth year of Jehoiakim son of Josiah, king of Judah (that is the first year of Nebuchad-
2 rezzar king of Babylon). This is what the prophet Jeremiah
3 said to all Judah and all the inhabitants of Jerusalem: For twenty-three years, from the thirteenth year of Josiah son of Amon, king of Judah, to the present day, I have been receiving the words of the LORD and taking pains to speak
4 to you, but you have not listened. The LORD has taken pains to send you his servants the prophets, but you have
5 not listened or shown any inclination to listen. If each of you will turn from his wicked ways and evil courses, he has said, then you shall for ever live on the soil which the
6 LORD gave to you and to your forefathers. You must not follow other gods, serving and worshipping them, nor must you provoke me to anger with the idols your hands
7 have made; then I will not do you harm. But you did not listen to me, says the LORD; you provoked me to anger with the idols your hands had made and so brought harm upon yourselves.

8   Therefore these are the words of the LORD of Hosts:
9 Because you have not listened to my words, I will summon all the tribes of the north, says the LORD: I will send for my servant Nebuchadrezzar king of Babylon. I will bring them against this land and all its inhabitants and all these nations round it; I will exterminate them and make
10 them a thing of horror and derision, a scandal for ever. I will silence all sounds of joy and gladness among them, the voices of bridegroom and bride, and the sound of the

handmill; I will quench the light of every lamp. For 11
seventy years this whole country shall be a scandal and a
horror; these nations shall be in subjection to the king of
Babylon. When those seventy years are completed, I will 12
punish the king of Babylon and his people, says the LORD,
for all their misdeeds and make the land of the Chaldaeans
a waste for ever. I will bring upon that country all I have 13
said, all that is written in this book, all that Jeremiah has
prophesied against these peoples. They will be the 14
victims*a* of mighty nations and great kings, and thus I will
repay them for their actions and their deeds.

✲ Ch. 25 clearly comprises two main sections, verses 1–14
and 15–38. The first of these forms a concluding summary to
the first part of the book as a whole, 1: 1 – 25: 14, the main
theme of which is judgement against Israel and Judah. As we
shall see, verses 15–38 belong to a separate section of the book,
the oracles against foreign nations, which are now contained
in chs. 46–51 in the Hebrew Bible but which originally
probably followed immediately after 25: 38.

Verses 1–14 are composed in the characteristic prose style of
the book and form another 'sermon', a number of examples
of which we have already come across. There can be little
doubt that this 'sermon' is a purely editorial composition
written by a Deuteronomic author as a summary conclusion
to the first major section of the book. It contains a number of
typically Deuteronomic words and phrases as well as other
Deuteronomic features (see the notes below). In addition, it
conforms to the same pattern which we have observed to
underlie other similar 'sermons' (cp. the comments on chs. 7,
11, 17, pp. 75f. 107ff. 152f.). Thus after an introduction in verses
1–2 it contains (*a*) a brief *résumé* of the word of God proclaimed
to Judah by Jeremiah and the prophets (verses 3–6); (*b*) a state-

[*a*] They...victims: *prob. rdg.; Heb.* They were the victims.

ment of Judah's rejection of, and disobedience to, that word (verse 7); and (c) an announcement of impending judgement upon the nation (verses 8–11). (On verses 12–14 see the notes.)

1. *in the fourth year of Jehoiakim:* that is, 605/4 B.C., which was the *year* in which Jeremiah dictated to Baruch a scroll containing the oracles which he had proclaimed during his ministry up to that time (cp. verse 3). A narrative describing the compilation of that scroll and the incidents the reading of it sparked off is contained in ch. 36. *that is the first year of Nebuchadrezzar king of Babylon:* in the Babylonian calendar the year began in the spring (about our April) and if a king came to the throne after the beginning of the year his first regnal year began the following spring, that is, at the next new year. Nebuchadrezzar became *king* about halfway through the year 605/4 B.C. which means that his first official regnal *year* began with the new year in 604 B.C. The period before this during which he had come to the throne was designated officially in Babylon as the accession year. Strictly speaking, therefore, 605/4 B.C. was not his first year but his accession year.

3. *For twenty-three years, from the thirteenth year of Josiah:* the same date for the beginning of Jeremiah's ministry is given in 1: 2.

4. *The LORD has taken pains to send you his servants the prophets:* here as elsewhere in prose passages in the book, the Deuteronomic author alludes to the word of *the prophets* sent by God to warn and exhort his people down through the centuries and the persistent rejection of their message by the nation (cp. e.g. 7: 25; 26: 5; also 2 Kings 17: 13).

9. *I will summon all the tribes of the north:* the 'foe from the north' is specifically identified in this verse with the Babylonians. As we have seen, it now seems very unlikely that the oracles in the book relating to the 'foe from the north' originally had in mind the Scythians. *my servant Nebuchadrezzar:* needless to say, the *king of Babylon* was not a worshipper of Israel's God Yahweh. Clearly he is here, as also in 27: 6 and

43: 10, referred to as *my servant* because he was the instrument of God's judgement upon Judah. The Septuagint omits this title for *Nebuchadrezzar* in all three texts in which it occurs, probably because a scribe or translator objected to the designation of a pagan *king* by so honourable a title.

and all these nations round it: since the 'sermon' clearly concerns Judah's apostasy and the judgement this was to bring upon them, this reference to the surrounding *nations* appears rather abruptly here and is probably to be regarded as a gloss which arose under the influence of verses 15–38 which do relate specifically to *these nations* (see also the comments on verses 12–14 below).

11. *For seventy years:* this number, which also occurs in 29:10, was not meant to be taken literally, as though the punishment (the exile) was to last precisely *seventy years*. The figure, which is found also used for a period of exile in texts from elsewhere in the ancient Near East, was a round or 'perfect' number and meant simply a long or very long time. *these nations shall be in subjection to the king of Babylon:* for the same reasons noted concerning the phrase 'and all these nations round it' in verse 9 above, this phrase here is also probably a gloss, an editorial expansion prompted by the contents of verses 15–38. Note that the Septuagint reads 'and they (that is, the people of Judah) shall serve among the nations seventy years'.

12–14. Since an oracle of judgement announcing *Babylon*'s overthrow is scarcely in place at this point, it is probable, as most commentators agree, that these verses are for the most part an editorial insertion into the original text of this chapter. The Septuagint concludes the 'sermon' with verse 13 *a: I will bring upon that country all I have said, all that is written in this book.* It is also possible that verse 13 *b: all that Jeremiah has prophesied against these peoples* was originally a superscription to verses 15–38. Probably, therefore, we should omit verse 12 and (with the Septuagint) verse 14 as secondary insertions, take verse 13*b* to have originally been the heading of verses

15–38 and regard verse 13*a* as having originally followed immediately after verse 11 (from which we have omitted 'these nations shall be in subjection to the king of Babylon'). Thus the discourse in verses 3–13*a* would originally have ended: 'For seventy years this whole country shall be a scandal and a horror; I will bring upon this ('this', referring to Judah, rather than 'that', referring to Babylon) country all I have said, all that is written in this book.' ✳

THE LORD'S CUP OF WRATH

15 These were the words of the LORD the God of Israel to me: Take from my hand this cup of fiery wine and make
16 all the nations to whom I send you drink it. When they have drunk it they will vomit and go mad; such is the
17 sword which I am sending among them. Then I took the cup from the LORD'S hand, gave it to all the nations to
18 whom he sent me and made them drink it: to Jerusalem, the cities of Judah, its kings and officers, making them a scandal, a thing of horror and derision and an object of
19 ridicule, as they still are: to Pharaoh king of Egypt, his
20 courtiers, his officers, all his people, and all his rabble of followers, all the kings of the land of Uz, all the kings of the Philistines: to Ashkelon, Gaza, Ekron, and the rem-
21 nant of Ashdod: also to Edom, Moab, and the Ammonites,
22 all the kings of Tyre, all the kings of Sidon, and the kings
23 of the coasts and islands: to Dedan, Tema, Buz, and all
24 who roam the fringes of the desert,*a* all the kings of
25 Arabia*b* living in the wilderness, all the kings of Zamri,
26 all the kings of Elam, and all the kings of the Medes, all

[*a*] who roam...desert: *or* who clip the hair on their temples.
[*b*] *So Sept.; Heb. adds* and all the kings of the Arabs.

the kings of the north, neighbours or far apart, and all
the kingdoms[a] on the face of the earth. Last of all the king
of Sheshak[b] shall drink. You shall say to them, These are 27
the words of the LORD of Hosts the God of Israel: Drink
this, get drunk and be sick; fall, to rise no more, before
the sword which I am sending among you. If they refuse 28
to take the cup from you and to drink, say to them, These
are the words of the LORD of Hosts: You must and shall
drink. I will first punish the city which bears my name; 29
do you think that you can be exempt? No, you cannot be
exempt, for I am invoking the sword against all that
inhabit the earth. This is the very word of the LORD of
Hosts.

⁂ In content 25: 15–38 is clearly closely related to the oracles
against foreign nations in chs. 46–51. The Septuagint places
these oracles after 25: 13a (omitting verse 14) and concludes
them with 25: 15–38 (= 32: 1–24 in the Septuagint). On
these grounds it is probable that the oracles against foreign
nations belonged originally with 25: 15–38, though it is more
likely that the latter formed the introduction to these oracles
and not a conclusion to them, as in the Septuagint.

The prose passage in verses 15–29 is easily recognized as a
separate unit from the largely poetic passage which follows it
in verses 30–8, though both passages have it in common that
they announce what amounts to judgement upon the whole
earth. Verses 15–29 are composed in the characteristic prose
style of the book of Jeremiah. They probably owe their
composition to Deuteronomic authors, though it is possible
that verses 15–16 come from the prophet himself and formed
the original nucleus of the present passage. Since Babylon
appears to be the dominant ruling power (cp. verse 26), it is
probable that the passage derives from the period before the

[a] So Sept.; *Heb. adds* of the earth.   [b] *A name for Babylon.*

conquest of Babylon by the Persian king Cyrus in 539 B.C. Of the nations mentioned in verses 19–26, Egypt, the Philistines, Edom, Moab, the Ammonites, Tyre and Sidon, Elam, the Medes and Babylon (= Sheshak; see the note on verse 26) are all referred to in chs. 46–51.

15. *this cup of fiery wine:* this cup is alluded to again in 49: 12, whilst in 51: 7 Babylon is referred to as 'a gold cup in the LORD's hand to make all the earth drunk'. Several passages in other writings from the same period also employ the *cup* as a symbol of God's wrath and judgement (Isa. 51: 17; Lam. 4: 21; Ezek. 23: 32; Hab. 2: 16).

18. *to Jerusalem, the cities of Judah:* God's own people are the first to receive the divine judgement (cp. verse 29).

19. *Pharaoh:* the Egyptian word means literally 'the great house' but gradually became the title for the king himself.

20. *all his rabble of followers:* literally 'all the mixed company', probably a reference to foreigners resident in Egypt and under Pharaoh's rule. *Uz:* the land where Job is said to have lived (Job 1: 1). Its precise location is not known but the indications are that it lay in the territory east of Palestine. *Ashkelon, Gaza, Ekron, and the remnant of Ashdod:* the main cities of the Philistines were the four here mentioned and Gath. The absence of Gath from this list is probably because it had long since declined (cp. also Amos 1: 6ff.). *Ashkelon, Gaza* and *Ashdod* have been identified with the towns bearing the same names today, but the sites of both *Ekron* and Gath have not been certainly identified. According to Herodotus, *Ashdod* was conquered by Pharaoh Psammetichus I after a very long siege in the seventh century B.C. This conquest with its consequent horrors for the population may lie behind the reference here to *the remnant of Ashdod.*

22. *the coasts and islands:* probably a reference to the colonies of *Tyre* and *Sidon.*

23. *Dedan, Tema, Buz:* the first two here mentioned are in north-west Arabia. The location of *Buz* is unknown but the fact that it is mentioned alongside *Dedan* and *Tema* probably

indicates that it also was in north-west Arabia. *all who roam the fringes of the desert:* see the note on 9: 26.

25. *Zamri:* where this was is unknown. One suggestion is that it should be identified with a place called Zabram known to have been located somewhere along the shore of the Red Sea west of Mecca. The Septuagint omits any reference to it.

26. *Sheshak:* also mentioned in 51: 41, this was a way of referring to Babylon by means of a device known as 'Atbash' whereby a consonant in the Hebrew alphabet is replaced by the corresponding consonant numbered from the opposite end of the alphabet. Thus the first consonant *aleph* (') is replaced by the last *tau* (*t*) or *vice versa*, the second consonant *beth* (*b*) by the second last, *shin* (*sh*), and so forth. By such means the consonants of the Hebrew word for Babylon, *bbl*, become *shshk*. The use of such a device in this instance probably points to a period when Babylon was still the ruling power, that is, to the time before 539 B.C. After that there would have been little reason for referring to Babylon in such a cryptic manner. ✷

UNIVERSAL DEVASTATION

Prophesy to them and tell them all I have said: 30

The LORD roars from Zion on high
and thunders from his holy dwelling-place.
Yes, he roars across the heavens, his home;
an echo comes back like the shout of men treading
        grapes.
The great noise reaches to the ends of the earth   31
        and all its inhabitants.
For the LORD brings a charge against the nations,
he goes to law with all mankind
and has handed the wicked over to the sword.
    This is the very word of the LORD.

32   These are the words of the LORD of Hosts:
        Ruin spreads from nation to nation,
      a mighty tempest is blowing up from the ends of
            the earth.

33   In that day those whom the LORD has slain shall lie like
        dung on the ground from one end of the earth to the
        other; no one shall wail for them, they shall not be taken
        up and buried.

34   Howl, shepherds, cry aloud,
          sprinkle yourselves with ashes, you masters of the
            flock.
        It is your turn to go to the slaughter,*a*
          and you shall fall like fine rams.*b*
35   The shepherds shall have nowhere to flee,
          the flockmasters no way of escape.
36   Hark, the shepherds cry out, the flockmasters howl,
          for the LORD is ravaging their pasture,
37   and their peaceful homesteads lie in ruins beneath his
            anger.
38   They flee like a young lion abandoning his lair,
          for their land has become a waste,
        wasted by the cruel sword*c* and by his anger.

   *   The theme of universal judgement in verses 15–29 is here
continued but without reference to the specific nations and
peoples referred to in the preceding passage. Whilst it is not
impossible that Jeremiah himself proclaimed such universal

               [a] *So Sept.; Heb. adds an unintelligible word.*
               [b] fine rams: *so Sept.; Heb.* a fine instrument.
               [c] sword: *so some MSS.; others* heat.

                            216

judgement, many commentators believe that this passage derives from a later author.

30. *The LORD roars from Zion:* this verse may be compared with Amos 1:2.

31. *For the LORD brings a charge against the nations:* the terminology of a lawsuit is again employed as it was in earlier chapters such as ch. 2.

34. *sprinkle yourselves with ashes: ashes* were sprinkled on the body as a sign of mourning, grief or humiliation. They are often mentioned together with dust and sackcloth.

35. The *shepherds* and *flockmasters* here mentioned are the rulers and kings of the nations. ✻

A NOTE ON FURTHER READING

Other recent commentaries on the book of Jeremiah are J. Bright, *Jeremiah* (The Anchor Bible, Doubleday, 1965), which contains an extensive introduction to the book and the life and times of Jeremiah, and J. P. Hyatt, 'Jeremiah – Text, Exegesis, and Exposition', *The Interpreter's Bible*, vol. 5 (Abingdon, 1956). A shorter but useful commentary is that by H. Cunliffe-Jones, *Jeremiah: God in History* (S.C.M. Torch Bible, 2nd ed., 1966). Older but still very useful are A. S. Peake, *Jeremiah*, vols. 1 and 2 (The Century Bible, Edinburgh, 1910–11) and A. W. Streane, *The Book of the Prophet Jeremiah together with The Lamentations* (Cambridge, 1913). J. Skinner, *Prophecy and Religion: Studies in the Life of Jeremiah* (Cambridge, 1922, paperback ed. 1961) remains a classic. The chapter on 'The Age of Jeremiah' in G. von Rad, *Old Testament Theology*, vol. 2, translated by D. M. Stalker (Oliver and Boyd, 1965), pp. 188–219, is characteristically perceptive and stimulating. On the problem of the prose sections in Jeremiah see the detailed discussion in E. W. Nicholson, *Preaching to the Exiles: A Study of the Prose Tradition in the Book of Jeremiah* (Basil Blackwell, 1970). For a more detailed description of the historical background to the life and times of Jeremiah, J. Bright, *A History of Israel* (2nd ed., S.C.M., 1972) and M. Noth, *The History of Israel* (2nd ed. with a revised translation by P. R. Ackroyd, A. and C. Black, 1960) may be consulted.

INDEX

Abarim, 187
Abiathar, 20
Abraham, 49
Adonijah, 20
Ahab, 165
'Ain Karim, 67
Amel Marduk, see Evil-merodach
Ammonites, 7, 98, 119, 214
Amon, 2, 19
Amos, 65, 67
Amyitis, 175
Anat, 79
Anata, 20
Anathoth, 1, 19, 20, 114, 115
apostasy, 31
Aramaeans, 7, 119
Ark of the Covenant, 45, 46, 78
Artemisia, 95
Ashdod, 214
Asherah, 149
ashes, 217
Ashkelon, 214
Ashtoreth, see Astarte
Assurbanipal, 2
Assyria, 2, 35, 48
Astarte (Ashtoreth), 79
astrology, 101
'Atbash', 215

Baal, 4, 37, 40, 49, 59, 128
Babylon, 1, 2, 7, 8, 62, 119, 214
Babylonians: as astrologers, 101; the foe from the north, 5, 7, 27, 127
Baruch, 7, 10, 12, 14
Bashan, 187
Ben-hinnom, Valley of, 37, 83, 162, 163
Benjamin, tribe of, 66, 154
Benjamin Gate, 153
Beth-Anathoth, see Anathoth
Beth-hakkerem, 67
Book of the Covenant, 109
burden of the Lord, the, 202
Buz, 214

Canaan, 3, 17, 29, 152, 182
Carchemish, battle of, 7, 35, 127
circumcision, 49, 98
cisterns, 33
Coniah, see Jehoiachin
covenant between God and his people, 18, 108–10
Cowper, William, 92
creation, myths about, 63
Cyprus, see Kittim
Cyrus, 175, 214

Dan, 55, 89
David, 15, 19, 178
Davidic kings, 178
Dead Sea Scrolls, 15
Decalogue, the, 76, 153
Dedan, 214
deliverance from Egypt, 32
Deuteronomy, 2–3, 71
dreams, 200

Edom, 8, 98, 214
Egypt, 1, 3, 35, 214; backs Zedekiah, 9; defeated by Babylonians, 7; practice of circumcision, 98
Ekron, 214
Elam, 214
Eli, 20, 78
Eliakim, 5
Elisha: call to be a prophet, 23; on Mount Carmel, 59; relations with Jehoash, 165
Esau, 93
Euphrates, river, 7, 35, 121
Evil-merodach, 175, 182, 189
exhortations to Israel and Judah, 27
exile, the, 1, 19, 189
Ezekiel, 20; call to be a prophet, 23, 25; symbolic actions, 165; vision of, 204
Ezra, 20

fertility rites, 37, 42
firstfruits, 29